'We put them all together on a big sheet of cardboard. I've got a black pen and we cross out every face that will fail. Ninety-five per cent of the time we're right. It's interesting to see them fall. Sometimes we put money on it. I can even tell when some of them will go. You can look at a man and say, "He'll fail on weekend four, he'll fail on Long Drag and he'll fail on TQ." You escaped the black pen, but Sampson is a surprise. We thought he'd fail. Most muscle men do.'

SAS Instructor

Adam Ballinger has worked as a management consultant. He has travelled extensively in Asia. In 1989, he joined the British Army as a reserve soldier.

THE QUIET SOLDIER

....

Adam Ballinger

ORION

An Orion paperback
First published in Great Britain
by Chapmans Publishers Ltd in 1992
This paperback edition published in 1994 by Orion Books Ltd,
Orion House, 5 Upper St Martin's Lane, London WC2H 9EA

A CIP catalogue record for this book is available from the
British Library.

ISBN: 1 85797 158 2

Printed in England by Clays Ltd, St Ives plc

Dear J,

You used to ask me searching and difficult questions which I evaded: Why are you always so tired? Why won't you talk about it? Why don't you give it up? At the time, I could find no answers. Indeed, I was frustrated by my own lack of understanding. But now that we are married, I want to give you the answers. They are in the pages that follow. I dedicate them to you, for you have forced me to sort out in my own mind a life that has dominated, at such cost to us both, the last two years.

With love,
A.

CONTENTS

A BIT OF ENGLAND

'I am ruminating,' said Mr Pickwick, 'on the strange mutability of human affairs.'

I rolled over and felt the crisp frost on the grass. The freshness stung my senses and opening my eyes I saw a clear blue sky. Long shadows, shortening with time, stretched out across the white sparkling hillside. Sunlight and shadow were already competing for space. Soon the sun would win and the icy white fields would become green once more.

As I lay on the grass, watching the sun slowly climb up into the sky, I knew that this was where I wanted to be. England was home and I was lucky to be here. I wanted to see the best of it before more fields were bulldozed away, before more roads were widened, and in case I never had the opportunity again. My destination was Scotland, more than three hundred miles to the north; and I was going to walk there, over the Pennines, from Alstonefield in Derbyshire.

An hour or so later, as I slipped into and out of sleep, I became dimly conscious of a voice calling.

'Mornin',' it said.

I sat up and looked around.

'Mornin',' it said again.

I turned and saw behind me a large man peering over a drystone wall. Black plastic sheeting was wrapped around his body and tied in place with coarse string.

'Where are you off to?' he asked, his breath condensing in the air.

'Scotland, eventually.'

'H'm. Long way.' He picked up his spade and walked off.

I stood up, leant against the wall, and watched him digging small holes in the adjoining field.

'What are you doing?' I called, intrigued by his actions.

'Trying to get rid of these moles.' He pulled a poisoned worm from his pouch and dropped it into the hole he had just dug.

'Destructive little blighters.' And then he turned his back on me and carried on working.

I left my rucksack propped up against the wall and walked down the valley to the river at the bottom. I crouched down beside a small plunge pool and filled my water-bottle. The clear water glistened in the sunlight.

'What will you do in England, sir?' Hassan asked, breaking the silence.

'I shall go walking in the hills while I still can.'

'Will you drink the streams, sir?'

'You remember?'

'Yes, sir, everything. Will you remember me?'

'Of course,' I said. 'You know that's a stupid question.'

I walked all day. The landscape was not new to me but I looked through new eyes, thankful eyes. I watched the clouds, and as they changed so did the colour of the moors, the peat hags and the rolling hills. There were drystone walls, farm buildings, church spires, graveyards and flowers.

Several days later I walked into a small town in the Yorkshire Dales. There was not much there; no great architecture, just a few slate-roofed houses arranged, with small alleyways, along a main road; and yet, in the drizzling rain, it looked charmingly drab. I splashed along the road towards the large guest-house at the end.

I walked across the lawn and up onto the white terrace. Behind me an elderly gardener, crouching over a pair of oily shears, was clipping the well-watered grass. Three or four other gardeners sat on their heels, their shoulders inches above their knees, around a growing pile of grass cuttings. Another, in a soiled white lungi, his wet skin shining, stood watering the flowerbeds with a large canvas hose-pipe.

I tried the door but it had been bolted from the inside. I knocked on the wooden panels, but there was no answer. When I banged again the door rattled, eerily, on its hinges. I hit it hard, and the hollow thuds rang out across the lawn. The gardeners had stopped their work. I could hear, over the dunes, the sea and the wind, but beyond that there was nothing.

The door opened slowly.

'You all right?' I asked.

Eyes yellow with jaundice stared at me.

'You asleep?'

'Yes, sir,' he said softly. The glaze slowly faded and I could see that he remembered me once more. He let go of the doorknob and turned to go back to his bed. Hassan moved awkwardly: he had taken a variety of drugs for eighteen years. Five or ten years ago he could not see his veins. Now they bulged like wires from his shrunken skin. I followed his bare feet across the dusty linoleum floor. They stopped at the side of his bed. He put his hand on the mattress to steady himself.

'I thought we'd go home.'

'Dhaka?' He raised his eyes from the floor and looked at me.

'Well, yes. Dhaka first, and then I'll go home.'

'Home?'

'Yes, England.'

He stood still, frail and sad in that sparse room. 'You don't want to go to Teknef?'

'No,' I replied. 'Not now. Do you?'

'No, sir.'

He let his head fall again and my heart sank. A translucent salamander clung to the wall, its heart visible and beating. I turned and closed the door.

*

As I sat in front of the tall fireplace, talking to the only other resident, who was an Anglican vicar from Kent, a man with a pale skin came in to light the fire. His shirt and woollen pullover were in tatters and his jeans held together by black masking tape. He had a very short haircut and a long, unkempt beard. When he saw us he nodded slightly. The little, grey-haired clergyman tried to draw him into our conversation, but he seemed disinclined to talk. He poked the cold ashes around for a while and then re-laid the fire.

'Walking?'

'Yes,' we both said, simultaneously.

'I started the Pennine Way once,' he added, 'but gave up when I got here.'

'Do you live here?' I asked, hoping that if he did, he would be able to tell me something about the house.

'Sort of. I live outside. I've converted the potting shed. I live there.'

'Good gracious.' The clergyman clasped his clean hands. 'Well I never.'

The young man crouched down on his knees, stretching the masking tape holding his trousers together, and put a match to the fire.

'I do the odd jobs. I like it here. I've been here eighteen months now.'

'Good for you,' said the clergyman, picking up his teacup and saucer.

When the fire was going he left us.

For a while my fireside companion kept saying, 'Extraordinary . . . Extraordinary.' But later, dazed by the warmth of the fire, he fell asleep in his chair. It was Hassan's habit to smoke at this time of day, and it was in the evenings when we sat and talked alone.

I opened the french windows and took a cane chair out onto the tiny balcony. Hassan got up from his bed and followed me. For a long time we sat listening to the waves crashing on the beach. A cool breeze flapped my shirt.

'What are you thinking about, sir?'

'I was thinking about this morning.'

'I don't like, any more, to fight, sir. This is very nice; so quiet now.'

'Yes,' I said. 'It's very peaceful.'

'When shall we go, sir?'

'I thought we might start tomorrow.'

'Chittagong?'

'Yes. But by bus.'

He smiled. 'No more boats then; not if we are going home.'

The sun was falling, soon it would reach the horizon. Groups of Bengalis still stood on the beach, their laughter carried on the wind.

I sat on my chair and looked down at my hands, unwashed since the handling of oily weapons in the bazaar.

'Can I see your palm, sir?' Hassan had seen me looking at my fingers.

'Here.' I held out my right hand.

He put his hand alongside and the contrast was all too obvious. Mine was white, much bigger and outwardly stronger. His was brown, small and withered.

'You are a strong man, sir. A lucky man. You enjoy a long life . . . Seventy or eighty years.'

The top line on my palm, he said, indicated one very strong marriage.

'You will marry only once, sir.'

Hassan showed me his hand. 'Look,' he said, pointing to a line with his left forefinger, 'three children, and one will die.'

Hassan took a cigarette out of the packet he concealed in his lungi. I watched him unroll it and scrape the tobacco into a small pile on the table. He added some brown powder that he kept wrapped in a small piece of paper. Slowly, and carefully, he mixed the two ingredients together between his forefinger and thumb. The wind caught a few leaves of tobacco and they fluttered across the table. Using his little finger he pushed the combination back onto the cigarette paper and rolled it up again.

'What can I do, sir?' he said, picking up his cigarette. 'I like this smoke.'

He struck a match, cupping the flame in his hands, then closed his eyes and breathed deeply. After a while he raised the cigarette to his lips again and inhaled. The wind dropped and the smoke rose slowly in the evening air. A lizard darted across the balustrade.

I tried to visualize him with his friends after a long day on his rickshaw. They would sit together in the tiny yard in front of his home, smoking and relaxing, away from the crowds; away from the police.

'What will you do in Dhaka?'

For a minute or two Hassan said nothing, but then he remembered.

'Go back to my rickshaw, sir.'

'And your wife?'

'Yes, sir. She has my daughter.'

Hassan's jet-black hair was greasy from neglect. He coughed painfully and, leaning over the side of his chair, spat out his phlegm onto the floor. He slouched back, and rolled the cigarette around between his fingers. Suddenly the smoke blew into his face and his eyes watered. He coughed again.

'Why did you come with me?'

'To travel with an honest man for the last time.'

'How did you know I was honest?'

'Your feet, sir.'

'Feet?' I laughed and looked at them. They were cumbersome, inelegant and dirty.

'And your face, sir.'

We sat quietly until we could see the sun no more. One by one the spectators left the sands and began their long walk home. A few remained, silhouettes against the sky. Soon they too would be gone.

Hassan put the cigarette to his mouth, inhaled deeply and then blew out the smoke. He extinguished the stub on the Formica table. 'I am so tired,' he said, getting up from his chair, 'I cannot talk. I am going to sleep now.'

As I walked I gradually became stronger. Day by day I increased the distances between my points of rest. One day, having spent the night in a vicarage, I set out with the intention of walking to a grange that had been recommended to me, forty miles to the north.

It was dusk before I finally limped, uncomfortably, into the estate.

I had just closed the gate when a tall man came striding towards me, crunching across the gravel in his well-made shoes. He smiled, and his narrow moustache seemed to lengthen sideways.

'Evening. You must be Ballinger. Come in. Come and meet my wife.'

Following him, I turned and caught one last glimpse of the farmyard. An old white Morgan had been parked in front of the barn. 'Nothing much here now,' he said. 'One or two rare breeds. Used to have a farm in Norfolk . . . A hundred acres. But retired now.'

We stepped inside and I changed for dinner.

I was admiring the oil paintings in his drawing room when he came in again. 'Ah, I see you're an artist. My wife does them in the winter. I frame them. Shockingly expensive to get them done. Poor job too.' At this, his wife emerged from the dining room with a bottle of sherry and three glasses on a tray.

'She sells a couple of dozen a year, don't you, dear,' he said, smiling at his wife. 'Mostly to Americans. Souvenirs of the grange. Bit of a cottage industry.' And his wife roared with laughter.

'She used to be a member of the Marine Artists in London, didn't you, dear . . . Suffolk Street, just behind the National Gallery, but not much marine scenery here. No sea.' And she laughed again.

The following morning as I sat outside on a wrought-iron seat, lacing my boots, I could see him strolling, quite happily, around his small estate. 'Had a good breakfast?' he said when he saw me. 'Good. Sets you up for the day. Going far? To Horton? Small place. Good walk, though. Twenty miles. Brave man. Well, all the best.'

When I left, he was pushing his white Morgan out of the barn and onto the gravel.

A few days later, I walked into Greenhead and ate in the Public

House. For an hour or so I was the only patron, but later, three pensioners came in and sat at my table. Disconcerted, for I was wrapped in my own thoughts, I went to the bar for another pint of beer.

'You're sitting in his place, you know,' said the barmaid.

'Whose?' I asked, surprised.

'The old man's.'

'Is it his?'

'Well, he's been sitting in that chair for fifty-two years.'

I went back to the table and apologized.

'It's all right. Sit down.' The old man patted the air with his muscular hand.

The elder two wore dark lounge suits, coloured shirts and ties. The younger man wore a tweed jacket and tie.

'First came here when I was twenty-one . . . Fifty-two years ago,' the old man said. 'Been coming here ever since . . . Except for the War. Six years in the Devon Artillery. Based in Plymouth. Dreadful people. Wouldn't even give you a boiled egg on your day off.'

He was a short, smiling, portly, red-faced Englishman; smoothly shaven and smart in his well-worn suit. He was disgusted with the selfishness of today's man.

'For six years I gave my life to this country. It's been buggered up. What a waste. All that life . . . Buggered up, I tell you. Disgraceful . . . Bloody disgraceful. Six years ago I was a draper. Forty quid a week. Never been on the Sick or the Dole in my life. Pension bigger than my salary now. You know what . . . I'll be the last man to be buried in Greenhead Church. Bought my plot in the sixties. Funeral will cost five hundred quid. Now, I ask you, how can a man on forty quid a week afford to die? It's bloody disgraceful, isn't it?'

Older eyes than mine looked at me pleadingly.

'Do you come here every day?' I asked, not caring what direction the conversation took.

'Do I like! Can't afford it. Wednesdays, Saturdays and Sundays. 'Course mild used to be a tanner a pint. Now a pound a pint. A pound a pint! Three pints and a whisky - to stop me getting up in the night - that's enough for me.'

The youngest of the three was the only one with a thick crop of hair. He used to delight in delivering newspapers to the vicarage when two pretty maids were employed there. 'Vicar was well-respected man, you know. Not now. These days we don't even have vicar in Greenhead. Vicarage is bed and breakfast. Times have changed, see.'

Two or three days later I walked into Bryness. I obtained the key for the sixteenth century chapel from a young girl in the adjacent garage. I sat quietly and alone in one of the pews, oblivious to the roar of traffic outside. I looked at the date on my watch and then realized that I had been in England for a whole month. I could see Hassan sitting on the balcony in Cox's Bazar.

'When I first saw my wife, I did not like her, sir.'

'Why?'

'She was only a girl. When we got married she was twelve years old. She was born after the fight for Liberation in 1971. I was given two rickshaws on our wedding day, but when I went out, later that week, she sold them for six thousand takka.'

'What happened to the money?' I asked.

'It was stolen. I needed money, too, sir. Man must have money.' Hassan raised his hands despairingly towards the sky, and then, as if the weight of his thought was too much for him, he dropped them again. 'All over the world, people think money, sir . . . Money very important, I know . . . But you are not like these people. I like this. You know, very well, Bangladesh, India, Pakistan . . . Very difficult countries.'

I listened carefully, but he seemed to lose the thread of his own thoughts. He was weak and tired easily. He sank further into the cane chair, his head resting against the curved back.

'Sir, I am very peaceful now. God knows about everything.'

The noise of the traffic had stopped. I stood up, and as I walked towards the entrance I noticed a leaflet that said that St Francis was

the Patron Saint. I opened the little door. A thrush swooped and
darted between two trees. In the graveyard several daffodils were
in bloom and the grass was neatly cut.

In the evening I dined with a soldier. I knew him by sight but
not by name, since we had met a few days previously on the
Pennine Way. Evasive about his past, I could gather only that he
had served with the Royal Engineers and the Parachute Regiment.
He was about five feet nine inches tall with short, grey hair. A
painfully sunburnt face told of a different climate. He was approaching his forty-fifth birthday and in a few days would retire
from full-time, active service. He walked with a curious loneliness.
His stride was always the same: he might just have walked ten miles
or thirty. It made no difference. I was always tired at the end of the
day and my legs ached if I walked much more than thirty miles. But
this indefatigable man seemed oblivious to distance. I warmed to
him because he was quiet and unassuming even though he was not
a man for anything but a factual conversation.

We talked about the next day. It was the last stretch to Scotland.
Twenty-nine miles over the Cheviot Hills with heavy packs. I
wanted to do it in one day and so did he. I knew it would hurt.

'I hope to start at seven o'clock,' I said, rotating my glass of beer.

'Do you? I'll start at seven-thirty.'

'We'll see who gets in first then,' I joked.

At seven-thirty the next morning I was sweating and climbing,
half an hour ahead of him. Thick, patchy mist swirled across the
summits for most of the day. Occasionally, when the mist did clear,
dark green hills stretched out in all directions as far as the eye could
see.

I crossed the agreed finishing line in Scotland a few minutes after
five o'clock, but, looking back, all thoughts of the race left me.
There behind me were three hundred miles of varied countryside.

The soldier came in just after seven.

The next day we travelled south together on the train. He was
going as far as Derby. I was going to Devon. We sat side by side at
a table in an empty carriage. I pulled a book from my rucksack and
placed it on the table. The soldier unfolded a simplified map of

England. It showed the long-distance footpaths. I started to read, but could not concentrate. I read and re-read the same pages over and over again. In the end I gave up. I wanted to talk to him but I did not know what to say. I looked across at his map. A yellow line ran, unhesitatingly, up the spine of England.

'I wonder how many people start the Pennine Way and do not finish it?' he said. 'You did well. Very well.'

'I enjoyed it,' I said, pleased that he had started the conversation. 'I like the hills and the moors. I enjoy tramping through peat bogs.'

He looked at me, and then I told him about Bangladesh and the Chittagong Hill Tracts. He appeared surprised.

'You went alone? You're a brave man.'

'No. A lucky man, maybe,' I added, remembering Hassan's words.

'I've been to Borneo,' he said, casually.

'What's it like?'

'Vicious. The grass is lethal: it's razor sharp.'

He showed me the palm of his hand. The scars remained but the lacerations had healed long ago.

'I have often thought about the army,' I said. I had, and I wanted him to tell me more, especially about himself. He looked around the empty carriage and out at the landscape rushing past. 'Then you should try the Reserve Special Air Service. They need good people.'

I laughed out loud. 'What about Long Drag?' I asked, trying not to be flippant. It was the only bit of their selection course I had heard about.

'You'll do it.'

Incredulous, I searched his face. 'Don't you have to run too?'

'Eight miles across country in an hour. It's easy.'

I thought of the worst terrain I could, and then tried to visualize myself running across it, in an hour, in a pair of old army boots. I couldn't.

'Where do you live?' he asked.

'London. Sometimes.'

'Here. I'll give you the phone number.'

He took out a black Biro and I handed him my copy of *Our Man in Havana*, the book I was trying to read. He scribbled the phone number on the inside of the back cover.

'Give them a ring. They'll tell you what to do.'

The train decelerated and ground to a halt in Derby.

'Shall I see you in London then?' I asked, as a parting gesture.

'Maybe.'

APRIL FOOL

For a young man who wants to enjoy himself, to spend a few years agreeably in military companionship . . . the British cavalry will be suited . . . To the youth who means to make himself a professional soldier, an expert in war, a specialist in practical tactics, who desires a hard life of adventure and a true comradeship in arms, I would recommend the choice of some regiment on the frontier . . .

Winston Churchill

I did nothing for four months. I did not dial the number because I did not know what it meant. I knew nothing about the army. I did not even know that a corporal was senior to a lance-corporal. None of my immediate family had been soldiers. Friends had served but that was different. Bravado prevented them from telling me what it was really like. 'It's good fun . . . You'll learn a lot about men . . . And yourself . . . It's tough . . . I was fit then . . . You'll laugh a lot . . . Like polishing boots do you?' And the SAS? This was not quite the army friends had described. I had read *Arabian Sands* and *Eastern Approaches* and knew that it was different, odd even. But that was all. What was it like today? What did they do? Was there a regular SAS and a reserve SAS? How were they organized? What sort of men did they want? More importantly, if I joined, what would I do?

I continued to hesitate. And then, one morning, spontaneously, and forgetting all rational deliberations, I dialled the number.

I was given a date, a time, a location and a kit list. The list was simple: something to run in and a pair of swimming trunks.

A few weeks later, on a sunny Saturday morning, I found myself with thirty other recruits warming up on the edge of a worn, wet and bumpy track for a five-mile run. The eight miles across country was to take place at some later date.

We were a motley collection of men, as different as men can be, brought together by a number, a date and a time. We hardly spoke.

Five miles in forty minutes. That was the time allowed. For the first three miles we had to stay behind a member of the regiment. He was a small man with short, thick, black hair. His eyes, which were a deep brown, were sunken so far back beneath his eyebrows that they were in shadow. He looked tired and he squinted in the sunlight. He leant forwards when he ran and took small but quick strides. A very thin line of perspiration ran down his spine and darkened his pale blue singlet, but otherwise he barely broke a sweat. His aim seemed to be to keep us only just jogging. There was a sharp, autumnal crispness in the air and a dusting of wet leaves lay on the track. Above the reassuring and rhythmic crunch of thirty people running in unison, I could hear the blackbirds in the trees. Suddenly he stopped and shouted, '*Run.*' I looked at my watch. He had left us eleven minutes to complete two miles.

Twelve completed in the required time and I was one of them. For some unknown reason, our swimming trunks were not needed. Twelve curiously diverse men then spent the rest of a bright morning in a dark and dirty shed, filling in coloured forms.

For six months nothing happened. I continued to train, but the security clearance did not come through. But then one week, quite suddenly, I was invited to attend for a medical, on April Fool's Day. When I arrived we were no longer twelve. Recruits from all over the south of England stood expectantly in front of a pair of green doors. I joined the crowd and tried, unsuccessfully, to pick out any of the original faces. Before long the doors were unbolted and we were led upstairs. Desks, cubicles and chairs filled a spacious hall.

I followed the others and sat down on one of the wooden benches.

One at a time, men were called up to a desk to answer a few questions, or to submit themselves to a test. Very few people spoke, other than to complain about the length of time the whole operation seemed to take. Every case caused confusion.

I turned to the man next to me and said, 'It's a shambles, isn't it?'

'Yes,' he said. 'I expected something a bit better than this, especially here. I thought these people would be more organized.'

'Everything seems to take so long.'

'Yes,' he replied, 'but that's the military for you. My name's Brown by the way.'

'I'm Ballinger. Can I have a look at your newspaper?'

'Of course,' he said, picking it up from the floor. As he bent down I could see that he was a tall, strongly built man. 'It's yesterday's *Telegraph*.'

'At least it's something to read. I expected to be out of here by midday. It looks as if we'll be here until six o'clock at this rate.'

'We'll get through eventually,' said Brown.

I opened Brown's newspaper, but found it difficult to concentrate. Everyone was getting restless and one or two people started talking. I listened, instead, to a conversation going on behind me.

'I've been on so many night marches, I've lost count,' the voice said. 'In 45 Commando—'

'What about kit, though?' interrupted his neighbour.

'Get the best. You want a razor-sharp knife. The sharper the better. I've got a small one, but it's bloody lethal. Get a bivvi bag. Not one of the smaller ones, but one of the bigger ones with a zip down the side. You want a small torch. And a map case. Get one of the big ones.'

'Have you done this sort of thing before?' said the inquisitive listener.

'Sure,' said the Commando. 'Too bloody often. I spent six years in the Marines.'

I looked at Brown and we both smiled.

'Have you ever parachuted before?' said the man next to the Commando.

'Fuck, yes. Forty-five, yes, about forty-five seconds before you hit the deck.'

Brown nudged me in the ribs and said, 'Go on, it's your turn.'

I walked up to the cubicle and a stocky man with a hard complexion took my blood pressure.

'One hundred and twenty over eighty,' he called out to his assistant, who transcribed the details into a table. 'Pulse: fifty-eight. Here, take this,' he said, passing me a plastic beaker, 'and go and piss in it.'

I took the vessel, walked behind the flimsy partition, and struggled to fill it to the half-way mark. I handed it back to the man who had taken my blood pressure.

'Jesus Christ!' he said, when I handed it back, 'we've got a right one here. I only wanted a few drops, not a bloody bucketful.'

He dropped litmus paper into the beaker and we watched it slowly change colour.

'Urine: pH seven,' he called out, and his colleague jotted down the details.

'Have you got a criminal record?' he asked.

'I don't think so,' I said. 'I don't know what you mean. Do you mean—'

'I mean,' he said, 'have you ever been summoned? Have you ever appeared in court? And before you say anything, it doesn't necessarily matter if you have. But you must tell the truth. Some blokes don't and then they're surprised, when the security clearance comes through, to find themselves off the course. I'll try again. Have you got a criminal record?'

'No.'

'Sure?'

'Yes.'

'OK. Go and sit over there and wait until the medic calls you.' And not giving me time to utter another word, he called out, 'Next.'

I sat down in front of another partition and waited for Brown.

'You were a long time,' I said, when Brown eventually joined me.

'It was the man in front of me. He had a pulse of eighty and the whole thing ground to a halt. No one knew what to do. He's probably not fit enough. Some people have got no idea. I don't know what they think they're trying to join.'

Towards the end of the afternoon, having had my photograph taken, I got bored with sitting down, and so placed Brown's newspaper on my seat and got up to stretch my legs. I was ambling around a large hall decorated with spectacular photographs, a Roll of Honour, a 21 SAS Regiment (Artists) Volunteers insignia, and a list of VCs, when somebody took me aside to repeat the Oath of Allegiance.

I was left alone with a captain in a small, scruffy room. He perked up when I came in, and stared at me beneath his black, bushy eyebrows. He sat behind a battered oak desk. Resting on the green leather top was a copy of the Oath, a black, cloth-covered Bible, and a pile of papers pouring over the edge of a wire tray. Behind him, a large map of the world had been pasted to the wall. Coloured pins had been pushed into different countries, and, in one or two places, they were clustered together. Above the map a four-foot scroll had been nailed lengthways along the picture rail. Written in black were the words, 'For many are called but few are chosen.'

'Sit down,' the captain said, when the door had been closed. He pointed to the chair in front of his desk. 'Why do you want to join?'

I muttered something about the purpose being worthwhile.

'How long do you expect to be with us?' he continued, not in the least perturbed by my reply.

'I'd like to think I would stay for at least five years. It's difficult to predict. Anything could happen.'

'Have you had the course explained to you?'

'No.'

'Right. I'll explain as much as you need to know at this stage. First, we begin with what we call Pre-Selection. It's a six-week training course. The purpose is to build you up for Selection. You'll train with us one evening a week. In between our sessions you have got to train on your own. This is not the regular army: we expect self-discipline. You have got to train in your spare time.

Exercise six days a week, and vary your routine. But, I warn you, when you train with us, don't get noticed and don't ever come last. If the corporals, who run the course, don't think you've got it in you, you won't even make it to Selection.

'Secondly, Selection – assuming you're still here. And I'll make that assumption. Listen carefully, very carefully.' He sat with his elbows resting on the desk and his hands together. 'You will make yourself available for alternate weekends for, at least, the next year, and for every drill night. Drill nights will be once a week. You will not miss one. There are no ifs and buts. That's it. Is that clear?'

I nodded.

He smiled, relaxed his shoulders, and sat back in his chair. 'You would not believe how many people come back asking for a weekend off. Girlfriends, funerals . . . I've had the lot. One bloke on the last course even tried to tell me his mother had died. I told him to bring her in, in a body-bag if he had to.

'Any questions?'

'No, I don't think so.'

'Good. There's a Bible. Repeat after me.

'I, Adam Ballinger . . .'

'Why did you come back at all?'

'Because, sir, Bangladesh is my country. I am a Muslim man. You cannot know about this . . . You don't know Bengali culture. I know Bengali mind, Bengali religion. I am a Muslim man, sir: I was born a Muslim man. I have Muslim blood in my body. You are a Christian man, sir: you have a Christian body, and Christian blood, Christian women, everything.'

'I, Adam Ballinger, Swear by Almighty God that I will be faithful and bear true allegiance to Her Majesty Queen Elizabeth the Second, Her Heirs and Successors and that I will as in duty bound honestly and faithfully defend Her Majesty, Her Heirs and Successors, in Person, Crown and Dignity against all enemies and will observe and obey all orders of Her Majesty, Her Heirs and Successors and of all the Generals and Officers set over me.'

When we had finished, the captain signed and dated my copy of the Oath.

'Here,' he said, passing it to me. 'Fill in your name and look after it. Pre-Selection starts next week. The corporals will give you the details. Can you make it?'

'Yes.'

'Good. That's what I like to hear. Maintain a sense of humour and you'll be all right.'

I smiled.

'Good luck with Selection,' he said, his eyes twinkling, 'and Ballinger—'

'Yes?'

'Send the next man in.'

RUNNING

One must try: one is not bound to succeed.
Frederic Manning

'OK. Listen in,' said the small corporal with the sunken, scrutinizing eyes. 'You. Yes, you in the green shirt. Ever heard of the grey man? Shut up and listen.'

All nervous, apprehensive laughter stops.

'This is Pre-Selection when we get rid of the no-hopers. And there are plenty of you. Wasters. I've no time for bloody wasters. For the next six weeks you'll train six days a week. Running, walking, cycling, swimming, weight-lifting, circuits . . . You'll do it all. This time, every week, you train with us. The rest of the time you train alone. Got it?

'OK. Let's go.'

We sprint out of the barracks and into the civilian world which I have only just left. Six soldiers run with us. The dark corporal sets the pace. A young girl, jogging in the drizzle, stands aside, frightened. It's cold.

We're running faster now and dodging parking meters, lampposts and police bollards. On and on. I glance at my watch. We've been running for thirty minutes. I'm soaked. Hot and wet. We are still running after an hour . . .

How long do we keep this up? My heart is thumping dangerously fast. I'm gasping for breath. Keep your head up. Breathe deeper. Keep up. Keep up. I can see nothing clearly. Louder grunts and gasps reach my ears.

'*Stop*. OK, adopt the press-up position.' Arms rigid but shaking. I close my eyes. My back rises and falls with convulsive breathing. 'Keep still. Down. With me. Up, down. Up . . . With me . . . Down. You. Shut up. Stop grunting. Up, down. Up, down . . . Come on, push it!'

'OK. Find yourselves a partner.'

No. Surely not more. I stand silent. The man next to me is my height.

'All right?' he asks.

'Yes.' Four hundred yards of wet, slushy sand lie before us. I try not to think about it.

'OK. In pairs . . . *Sprint*.'

What's happening to my legs? Each one wobbles. From the waist up I don't know what's happening.

'*Stop*. In pairs, into piggy-backs. *Wait!* You. What's your name?'

'Williams,' a voice says from behind me.

'Get over there, Williams, you're wasting my time. *Move!*'

Williams, caked in wet sand, stumbles out of the sand track and onto the grass. He is violently sick.

'The rest of you, listen in. That man there is a waster. A bloody waster. Anyone here want to join him? You! Yes, you in the red vest. Wanna stop?'

'No, staff,' a voice mutters.

What's he saying? I can't hear. My heart is thumping too loudly.

'OK, we'll try again. Into piggy-backs.'

My partner lifts me up onto his back. At last, rest. Breathe deeply.

'See that bin over there' – a red municipal rubbish bin lies on the edge of the sand one hundred and fifty yards away – '*Go!*'

'Go on. Keep it up. Push it. Push it. Excellent. You're doing well. Keep going. Excellent. Ten yards ahead of the rest. Beautiful. Keep it. Keep it. Beautiful.' I'm yelling with excitement into his ear.

'*Swap*.'

'God, you're heavy.'

'Run. Run.' He's on my back screaming at me but I can't hear properly. 'Run.'

We win. Rest. Thank God. Rest. The last man is coming in. Can't he go slower? We need more rest.

'Who's feeling ill? You. You're Jones, aren't you? All right, Jones?'

'No, staff.'

'*No?* What's the matter with you?'

'Done in, staff.'

'Done in! Now that's a pity. Isn't that a pity. Jones, find Williams. Go on. Piss off.

'Look. Two wasters already, lads. Any more?'

More sand stretches before us. Thank goodness it's raining. I'm burning hot.

'OK. In your pairs. Wheelbarrow races. Who doesn't know what a wheelbarrow is?'

Good, a demonstration. More rest. Breathe deeply.

'*Go.*'

I'm holding his knees and running. His hands and wrists have disappeared into the sand. He is jogging on his arms. We're doing well. We're near the front. I push him faster, but his arms pack up. I plough on pushing his face through the sand, his arms buckling beneath him.

'Swap.'

My turn. I'm running on my hands. My legs are in the air. Jesus. Help me . . .

'OK, lads, that's it out here. Now, a nice run back to the barracks.'

Thank goodness. It's over.

'*Sprint.*'

Am I conscious? I'm sprinting through wet, puddled, ankle-deep sand. I'm running to catch the man in front of me, but the sand is so soft. It's pulling at my feet like viscous glue. We are stretching out like a concertina. The corporal is increasing the pace. There are three men trailing him. They are a long way in front. More than a hundred and fifty men are struggling to catch them.

Suddenly the sand gets firmer. I try to run faster, but the sand goes soft again and I slow. I try another burst when it gets harder and catch the man in front. It's Brown. We look at each other. I force a smile, but Brown does not notice me: he is staring blankly at something. His head has fallen forwards as if it is too heavy for him.

I run on, trying to keep up with Brown. I can hear the footsteps of a man behind me.

'Been in the army before?' the soldier asks, as he runs up and down the column, like a sheepdog rounding up his flock.

'45 Commando,' says the man following me.

'Good,' says the soldier. 'Keep going. Go on. Catch that waster in front of you. He's slowing up now.'

The barracks. I've made it. Not quite. More sit-ups, press-ups, leg raises. Sprint a hundred yards, put your forefinger on the ground, run around it ten times, sprint back.

Wet. Caked in sand.

'It's all psychological, lads. Just a bit more. Teams of five now, lads.'

We shuffle into teams. The corporal looks tired but cruel.

'Come on. *Move it!* Jesus Christ. One stretcher per team.'

A dozen or more stretchers lie on the inside of the running track. I pick one up with the Commando. He is small and his biceps are disproportionately large. The weight surprises me. I thought stretchers were made of wood and canvas. These are rigid and made of steel. The base is a solid plank.

'One man on each corner,' the corporal in charge shouts, 'and a man on top. At the end of each lap, change round. It's a five-lap race. Any questions? *Go.*'

Commando is the smallest. He jumps on top and we lift him and the stretcher up onto our shoulders.

'Run,' Commando shouts. He is lying down and screaming into my ear. I am at the front, on the left. My right shoulder is killing me. 'Take it on the bone,' he says. 'On the bone. Muscle tires. Let it rest on the bone. In step. In step. Come on, boys. Catch those buggers. Keep in step now. Good. That's it. Come on. Left, right, left, right. Come on. Push it. Push it.'

We are sprinting towards the team in front. The stretcher is bouncing up and down on my shoulder bone. I hold the steel bar and try to cushion the blow, but it crashes down with every stride.

'Keep your head up!' Commando pulls my hair back to stop my head from falling forwards. '*In* through the nose. *Out* through the mouth. Come on.

'Excellent. Drop it. Just drop it.'

We let go of the stretcher. It crashes to the ground, with Commando still on top.

'On you get,' he shouts, and I lie on the stretcher.

My lap of rest is over too quickly. It's a blur. I can't see straight. I feel light-headed.

'Well done, lads,' says the corporal. 'I want one team of five now. You, yes you lot.' He points to us. 'See that red Toyota pick-up over there? Bring it here.'

I stare, incredulous and hesitant.

'*Run!* . . . Jesus Christ.'

We push it onto the running track.

'The rest of you adopt the press-up position. When I say go, you lot are going to push the Toyota around the track, and the rest of you are going to do press-ups until they get back here. Got it? Any questions?'

Four hundred yards on a gravel track. Not too bad. A soldier accompanies us, in the driver's seat. I am leaning against the tail-gate alongside Commando.

'Make sure that handbrake stays on.'

'OK.' The soldier smiles back at his boss.

'Go.'

This is the worst of all. I can't breathe. I can't swallow. My throat is totally desiccated. I'm drained. I'm done in. Two hundred yards. Half-way. Two hundred yards and it's all over. Just a bit more. Keep going. Keep going. Don't go down yet. Oh God. Don't swallow. Just push this van. Push. One hundred yards. Yes. There's the finish. I can't, I can't make it. Go. Yes. Nearly there. Don't stop. Push . . .

'Good effort, lads. That's it. See you next week.'

UNIFORM

*We not only look at things from different points
of view, but with different eyes; we do not care
to find them alike.*

Pascal

Six weeks later, along with the other survivors, I found myself
queuing up in a poorly lit concrete corridor to see the Storeman.
The grey skirting boards had been scuffed black with army boots.
I stood in the middle of the queue next to Brown. Commando was
at the back talking, audibly, to someone else.

'How did you find Pre-Selection?' I turned to Brown and asked.

'Terrible. I wondered, for a dreadful moment, if I'd made a
mistake.'

'It had its moments. What about the corporal who took us?'

'Which one?' he said, leaning back against the wall.

'The little one. The one with the sunken eyes.'

'Oh, him. That's Scott. He's attached to the Training Wing.
He'll be with us for Selection.'

'Have you been in the army before?' I asked, after the queue had
moved forwards two or three places.

'Yes, but not the regular army. I've been in the TA for six years.
I had to leave my old unit to try this. It'll be embarrassing if I
fail.'

'Do you know anyone else here?'

'I know Avery.' He pointed to a well-built, stocky man two

places in front of us. 'And I know Cordwell. We were in the same unit together.'

I recognized Cordwell when Brown pointed to him. He was the shortest man on the course. He had a chest that blew out like a barrel when he inhaled, and he could run very fast. Commando didn't like him.

'The numbers seem to have gone down already,' I said, standing out in the corridor.

'Yes, but that's not surprising. Half of them had no chance. One chap was puffing and wheezing after the first mile. The trouble with a unit like this is that it attracts the wrong sorts.'

The queue moved forwards slowly. One by one, men came back from the store laden with kit. When Brown disappeared inside, I stood at the front of the queue and looked in through the doorway. An old, grey-haired Storeman stood, like a shopkeeper guarding his supplies, behind a wooden counter. Grey steel shelving lined the square room. Scott clambered, in the background, from shelf to shelf, to retrieve each item as the Storeman called it out. He kept a list on his bench, and as Scott threw each item onto the floor the Storeman marked his records with a black pen. When he had finished with Brown he called me in.

As I stepped forwards he looked at me, made an estimate of my size, and then circled 'medium' on his schedule.

'Windproof smock,' he called out to Scott, and presently one landed on the floor behind the counter. The Storeman picked it up and passed it to me. The sequence continued: 'One windproof trousers. One green trousers. Two shirts, hairy. Two pairs of socks. One cap-comforter. One woolly-pully. Two mess tins. Two water-bottles. One belt. One poncho. One kit bag. One bergen. One pair of boots.'

He passed me the boots and smiled. They were a pair of wide fitting size 11s. The letter 'L' had been written in chalk on the toe caps. 'Sorry,' he said, 'I've run out of mediums.'

I walked back to the crowded changing room.

As I undressed I began to feel self-conscious. I had been given a pile of new clothing, but did not know how to wear it.

Commando, who had been the last man in the queue, but the first to change, saw me fumbling with the bottom of my trousers, and came striding across the congested changing room.

'Got any rubber bands?' I shook my head. He went back to his bag, rummaged through the contents, and came back with two bands.

'Have these. The postman puts them round our bills.'

He put the bands around my ankles and then, turning the trousers back up on themselves, tucked the ends in between the elastic and my leg. He pulled at the bottom of the trousers so that the crease dropped vertically, and stopped abruptly at the top of my boots. When he had finished, I showed him the green, elasticated, woollen tube that the Storeman called a cap-comforter. With a sequence of quick folds and tucks he converted it into a piece of headgear.

Dressed, I looked at the others and was struck by the transformation. Until a few minutes ago we had been wearing different civilian clothes. But now, all outward signs of individuality had gone. We stood in camouflage, concealed by each other.

Men meandered around the changing room laughing at their new, ill-fitting clothes. Dozens of others stood around three small mirrors checking their appearances. When I did the same I received a sharp shock, for this was more than a transformation of dress, and I felt uncomfortable. It was not that the uniform did not fit, or that I was one of many, for such things did not bother me. It was that I felt different. Nothing looked quite the same.

'Good,' said Commando, adjusting my cap-comforter until it met his exacting standards. 'Now you look like a soldier.'

An hour later we were on parade, in uniform, for the first time.

'Quite frankly, some of you are a disgrace. What's wrong with you? Are you queer?'

'No, sir.'

'One Squadron are you?'

'Yes, sir.'

'Thought so. You're all the same. *Stand up straight then!*'

The Sergeant-Major was perfectly cast. He was theatrical rather than real. An enormous waist prevented him from seeing the ends of his own ample boots. A huge, ruddy and puffed-out face, shaven as smoothly as a baby's cheek, hung as flab well below the bone in his chin. He held his giant swagger stick with more conviction, and more steadiness of nerve, than a heart surgeon holding a vital artery with a pair of forceps.

'You. Yes, you! You got a big dick or something?'

'No, sir.'

'Put your feet together then, not a yard apart.

'Next week I want you here for parade at seven o'clock. What does that mean?' His blue eyes ran rapidly up and down the ranks before coming to rest on Brown.

Brown sprang to attention. 'Eighteen fifty-five, sir!'

'Good. Everyone got that? Eighteen fifty-five. After parade you will proceed to your lessons.'

The OC handed the Sergeant-Major a list, which we had all signed, and he began to read out the names. He stopped at the second one.

'Who is Wool . . . Woe . . . Woo . . . I can't read this?'

'Wood, sir.'

'Wood, learn to write before next week.'

'Yes, sir.'

'Hey . . . And what have we got here?' The Sergeant-Major had spotted something in the second rank, and lowered his register.

The two scruffiest recruits, both wearing crumpled shirts, were standing together.

Delighting in his catch, he strode over to within an inch of them, and said, 'You two will share the cost of an iron before next week. Got it?' And then, tugging at their shirts, 'These are not horse blankets.'

During parade I hid myself firmly in the middle of the squad, for I could neither understand the monosyllabic screams that passed for commands, nor keep time, nor maintain a straight face. After a fashion I managed to synchronize my movements with everyone else's but only by being relatively relaxed. Avery, who was behind me, told me I was noticeably too relaxed; arms not straight but swinging gaily like those of an orang-utan.

Later we practised saluting; to the front, to the right and to the left. When we all saluted to the right one recruit, an ex-regular corporal, turned to the left. The OC who was watching this debacle smiled, but not the Sergeant-Major. His face turned the colour of a fire-extinguisher.

'*You!*' he screamed.

'Sir!' The corporal jumped to.

'What's your name?'

'King, sir.'

'King, you got a brain?' the Sergeant-Major asked disbelievingly.

'Think so, sir.'

'Think so!'

'I mean, yes, sir.'

'Next week, King, show me your right foot.'

'Sir.'

'The week after that show me your left foot . . . If you're still here. Got it, King?'

'Yes, sir.'

Parade was in turmoil. We had become a giggling mob.

'OK, lads,' the OC intervened. 'We don't do much drill in this regiment, but what we do do needs to be right. That's all.'

LESSONS

Now then boys, you have a week or two left.
Make the most of it. No preparation can be too
thorough for the life that awaits you; relentless;
the weakest to the wall.

Henry Williamson

'*Atten – – tion!*

'Stand at – – *Ease!*'

The Sergeant-Major, having issued his commands, took one step back across the parade-ground. The OC took over.

'Listen in, lads,' he said, walking forwards. 'I've got your numbers here. Engrave them on your memory. You will have them for life, or,' he added, smiling, 'for as long as you are here, which for most of you will not be very long.'

When he had read out all the numbers, he carried on. 'Listen in. The format for the next six weeks is as follows. Parade: nineteen hundred hours. The Sergeant-Major will take you, straight away, for fifteen minutes' drill. And I advise you,' he said, lowering his voice and grinning, 'to listen to him, very carefully. At nineteen-fifteen you will move, immediately, into your classrooms for the map-reading course. If, and only if, you pass the test at the end of the course, we let you out on the hills. And then all hell breaks out. Half of you will still get lost. At twenty-one hundred hours Corporal Scott will take you for PT. Any questions?'

No one spoke.

While Brown and I stood waiting to get into our designated classroom, the OC, who was standing in the doorway chuckling to himself, said, 'What do you think of the Sergeant-Major, then?' But before we had time to answer, he continued, 'He's not in the regiment now: he's retired. We let him wear his beret as a concession. He's superb, isn't he? Ruthless. We save him for the new recruits. Scares the life out of them.' As the OC spoke, I could visualize him unlocking a cabinet and wheeling out the Sergeant-Major, like a piece of priceless Georgian silver, reserved for special occasions. 'Don't upset him, whatever you do,' the OC added.

'At least PT will be shorter from now on,' Brown said, as he and I walked into the classroom.

We pushed our way through the clutter of desks and found two empty spaces a few rows from the back. The place was in near darkness and as dismal as an ageing schoolroom on a dank November day. A dim, solitary light bulb hung shadeless, from the middle of the ceiling. The desks were dusty and every one seemed to rock. We sat on shabby, plastic chairs. They too were stained. Scruffy, grey metal cupboards, with their identification numbers hastily painted on the back, stood idly about the room. A worn-out overhead projector was used to show damaged, black-and-white slides. They were invariably out of focus.

Every week Scott took the lessons. I had always considered my navigation to be excellent but this was different. Often we would be searching, we were told, for a cache no bigger than an ammunition box, buried underground. Despite his abrupt manner, Scott took great pains to teach us according to his manual. He was often, however, tired and short-tempered. His dark, darting eyes, hidden underneath his thick, black eyebrows, betrayed uneasiness. Rough skin, stretched tightly over hard, battered cheekbones, suggested a severe and mysterious lifestyle.

One week he arrived charged with anger. We sat obediently and quietly through the map-reading lesson trying desperately to avoid his stare. I kept my head down and took notes meekly. Only when our lesson was over, and we had changed for PT, did he vent his full frustration on us. He worked, we guessed, in the City of

London by day and loathed the experience. Perhaps the last eight hours had taxed his patience more than most for, in an hour and fourteen minutes, he paced us for thirteen miles around the streets of London. We ran around Battersea Park, St James's Park, Green Park and Hyde Park. After about the tenth mile, Avery and Brown began to drop back; and Scott suddenly shouted at Avery, treating him like a disobedient dog who refuses to move when told. Even Commando looked away.

'You enjoying it?' Scott scowled, knowing that he was hurting Avery more and more with every step we took.

'Yes, staff,' said Avery, in between his gasping breaths. And then with perfect equipoise added, 'We going around Regent's Park next, staff?'

As we moved, week by week, closer to the map-reading test I realized that I had learned nothing about the SAS, or even 21 SAS, the regiment I was trying to join. I had been swept along by the tide. We delighted in hearsay. Any man who knew anything, or even claimed to know anything, about the Special Forces was listened to assiduously. One recruit, who had once tried to join 23 SAS, said we would need stamina more than cardiovascular fitness. But no one admitted to knowing how Selection would really progress. Even Commando was evasive when I asked him. He was convinced, however, that the good recruits would be invited to join the regular SAS. The OC kept saying, 'It will all be explained in due course. All you have to do is pass what we throw at you. Don't go troubling yourselves with what's coming next.'

Feeling vulnerable, I did some research. There were two threads to the story: the Artist Rifles and the Special Air Service.

In 1800 Colonel Coote Manningham raised the Rifle Brigade; a unit of tough individuals each capable of operating alone and without orders. Unlike many other infantry regiments of that time, they wore a green uniform. In 1859, following the Crimean War and the Indian Mutiny, the British (Conservative) Government approved the Volunteer Movement when yet another war, this time with France, looked imminent. Twelve thousand men enrolled and, on 10 May 1860, one hundred and nineteen of these were attested with the 38th Middlesex (Artists) Rifle Volunteers. These men were artists, sculptors, musicians, writers and poets who enjoyed a cocktail of creativity and action. One of them was the Pre-Raphaelite, William Morris.

The Artist Rifles was mobilized on 3 August 1914. Wilfred Owen joined them, just over a year later, on 21 October 1915. By the end of the First World War one in fifteen of these men had won either a VC, a DSO, or an MC. The Artist Rifles' memorial plaque stands to the right-hand side of the entrance to the Royal Academy.

In 1945, along with many other units, the Artist Rifles were demobilized.

The Special Air Service, however, was not lost quite as quickly. Founded and led by David Stirling, they had achieved impressive results during the Second World War. Small parties of well-trained, disciplined and very determined men, operating behind enemy lines, had succeeded in inflicting a disproportionate amount of damage to alien airfields and supply depots. Numerous lessons had been learnt and, in November 1946, the War Office concluded that such experience should not be relegated to a filing cabinet, but instead should be kept alive, used and developed. Since a regular unit was not deemed essential in times of peace, a Territorial unit was approved, and this was the 21st Special Air Service.

In 1947, therefore, the wartime SAS regiment was reborn in a different guise. It needed to be attached to a regular parent unit and the Rifle Brigade was chosen. Subsequently, 21 SAS merged with the Artist Rifles and became as it now is: The 21st SAS Regiment (Artists) Volunteers. The headquarters are in the south of England.

In the 1950s, however, as a result of the Malayan Crisis, it became obvious that there was, once again, a requirement for a regular regiment. Consequently, a new regiment was born out of 21 SAS and this became 22 SAS. The 22nd Special Air Service is now the only regular regiment.

In 1959 a new Territorial Army unit, 23 SAS, was added in the north of England.

*

On the sixth week, after parade, we sat down to the map-reading test. Scott handed out scrappy sheets of faded foolscap paper, and read out twenty-five questions. For one or two of these he showed some map projections and we had to identify the salient features.

As I leant over my script, struggling to see properly in the half-light, Commando, who was sitting to my left, whispered, 'Come on. Move your arm. I can't see what you're writing.'

THE HILLS

*I will lift up mine eyes unto the hills, from
whence cometh my help?*

Psalm 121

Commando and I passed the map-reading test with scores that
differed by one mark.

We had passed the first written test and exercised vigorously for
three months, during Pre-Selection and during the map-reading
course, but Selection proper had not really begun. Now it did. For
the first time recruits associated with different squadrons from
across the south of England came together for Selection. Each
squadron had its own base and its own drill hall, but they all came
under the umbrella of 21 SAS. I, and about thirty others, had
applied to join One Squadron, but the total number of recruits for
21 SAS came to about one hundred and fifty.

We left the barracks, as a squadron, one sunny Friday evening,
and drove in four-ton trucks towards the west of England. It was
well past midnight when we finally stopped, with a jolt, in front of
a disused aircraft hangar. We jumped out, over the tail-gate and
onto the concrete. Rapidly moving clouds obscured the moon
from view. A pair of roving white searchlights scanned the
perimeter fencing, picking out nothing except barbed wire and
concrete posts. One or two diodes, fastened to the top of some
irregularly spaced aerials, glowed red in the darkness.

We filed into the open-ended hangar, the wind following us

inside. The Storeman gave each of us a mug of soup and an old
sleeping bag. One or two men were pacing around in the dim
electric light, carrying jerry cans and ammunition boxes. A small
portable generator rattled away in the corner. The OC sat on a
collapsible chair going through his papers. Every now and then a
gust of wind fluttered his notes. We were directed, as a squadron,
to a far corner of the hangar.

'Find yourselves some space, lads, and get some kip,' Scott said,
while standing among the other recruits who were already asleep
on the floor.

Reveille was at five o'clock. Minutes later the eight-mile run across
country began. It was not nearly so bad as I had imagined, for the
OC paced us and he made sure we took an hour, the allotted time,
and not forty-five minutes, just to be vindictive. Even at five
o'clock in the morning, when our senses were suddenly and cruelly
shaken into action, all but three recruits completed the course on
time.

After a brief parade and a rapid breakfast, we sat on benches in
the disused hangar and waited for the OC to address us.

Commando sat next to me. 'You all right?' I asked. 'Are you
limping?'

'Yes,' he said. 'Nothing much. I had a knee injury in the
Marines. I went to a military hospital and that was a bloody mistake.
I should have gone to a civilian doctor. They operated and made
it worse. Joint's not been right since. I try not to run. Circuit
training keeps me fit. You've got to push yourself till you're nearly
sick. I do it five days a week, sometimes six. Press-ups, squats, sit-
ups . . . You name it, I do it.'

'Are you going to be all right, though? There's going to be a lot
of running.'

''Course I fucking will.'

The OC stood up first and, standing on a platform behind a
lectern, formally introduced himself.

'I'm an officer in One Squadron, 21 SAS. The Training Wing
headquarters are at their barracks, and that's where I live. Those of

you trying to join that squadron will see a lot more of me than the rest of you. Sorry, lads, if you're going for One Squadron,' he said, grinning, 'you're disadvantaged. For the next two years I'm the officer in charge of 21 Selection, in all its phases. If you need to speak to me, you call me sir.'

The OC went on to explain the course.

'The purpose of this weekend, lads, is twofold. First, to introduce you to the course. It is designed for the man off the street: we assume nothing. The old soldiers among you will find it frustrating at times, but on others you will have the advantage. I make no apologies.

'The course is broken into three phases: Selection, Camp and Continuation, and to enter the SAS you have to pass every test within every phase. And I warn you,' he said, lowering his voice, his eyes flashing over the lectern, 'there's not a man in this regiment who would say it's easy.

'The second purpose of this weekend is to get rid of the wishful-thinkers, the no-hopers. Every man in the British Army has to pass basic tests. You've already done the eight-mile run. Expect more. They're not difficult, but some of you will fail them. Even as I speak, three blokes are on their way home. Sorry to disappoint you, lads. If you had your sights set on the underwater knife-fighting course, this weekend, forget it. That comes later.'

When the OC had finished, and the laughter on the benches had died down, he nodded to a bulging Falstaff-like figure standing in the shadow of the stage.

'I will now,' the OC said, 'hand you over to the PSI, or, to the civilians among you, the Permanent Staff Instructor. Listen, very carefully, to what he has to tell you.'

The OC took one step backwards. The instructor stepped up onto the stage and placed his notes on the lectern. He had a jet-black moustache which was as thick as the hair on his head. He was not as tall as the OC but he looked much stronger. As he spoke he seemed to swell out sideways, around the lectern. His eyes sparkled in the dim light and he smiled broadly.

'I spent twenty-one years in 22 SAS,' he said, 'and the last three running 22 Selection. I am attached for the next year to 21 SAS. I will be in the background on your drill nights and during every weekend. You may not notice me, but I'll be watching you. It's my job to assist the OC.'

When he had finished, the OC went on to explain the first phase of Selection. It would consist, he said, of nothing more than a series of marches with a rucksack, called a bergen, over the hills, followed by some PT. We would march first in squadrons, then in pairs, and finally alone. Each weekend the length of the marches would increase and the loads would get heavier. There would be few surprises. Nothing sinister, nothing beyond an ordinary, fit man with a brain, patience and self-discipline.

We could, the OC explained carefully, drop out at any time. Indeed failure was common: too common, he said. 'People leave because they lack fitness and endurance, because they lack incentive or aptitude, because they are injured and because, and it grieves me to say this, lads – because they give up.

'If you voluntarily withdraw, lads, you can never, and I mean never, serve with the Special Forces again. In plain English, don't bother coming back. VW's that simple. Any questions?'

Not a hand was raised.

'If you remember only one thing, lads, remember this: the object is to persevere and succeed in the aim. That's what it's all about. Failure is a disgrace.'

From now until Camp, he explained, during drill nights, our map-reading lessons would be replaced by weapon training, but on every alternate weekend we would be on the hills.

Later on, to my surprise, we had a lecture on the Country Code. 'It's your country, lads,' Falstaff said. 'Look after it. That's why you're here, isn't it?'

Only one person nodded. Undoubtedly more motives than this one filled the room.

After lunch the basic swim test began. The purpose was to see if we could swim, quietly and without panicking, three times around the edge of a very deep, cool pool. The OC had already told us that we would have to swim rivers, and that we would have to pass the thousand metres swim test, in combat clothing, before the end of the course.

We all had to queue up in the nude and this upset Commando. Falstaff stood at the head of the queue and made sure each man jumped, according to his instructions, without hesitation. There was a drop of five feet or more between the top of the water and the edge of the pool.

I stood alongside Brown. Suddenly the queue stopped moving. One man, three or four places in front, refused to jump.

'I can't swim,' he said.

But all Falstaff said was, 'OK. Go and get changed.'

Brown was far more surprised. 'It's astonishing, isn't it? Why bother to undress? Surely he didn't expect to get away with it. Fancy turning up for the course not being able to swim. It's a basic requirement. The money the army wastes on these people.'

Back in the training area we were confronted with the tunnels test. Falstaff stood on a steel drain cover on the edge of some boggy woods. Ditches and streams ran in a series of criss-crosses through a maze of fallen trees. On one side of the wood there was a large rectangular pond. A pipe, two to three feet in diameter, ran into the stagnant water, so that all but the top few inches was submerged. The distance between the water level and the top of the pipe would be just enough, if once inside it you twisted your neck to take a breath. The water, a muddy, mustard colour, lay still and silent. Green algae floated on the surface around the pipe's mouth.

The OC stood on another drain cover in the woods about a hundred yards away. Scott guarded another, among a tangled nest of briars and nettles, perilously close to the pond.

'Listen,' Falstaff said, smiling and tapping the drain cover with a long stick. 'A lot of what we do is in the dark, and in confined spaces. We cannot afford to have any Go Berserkers. This will sort you out.

'I am going to send you down one at a time. I shall tell you to go either to the OC or to Corporal Scott. Take a good look at them. Get your bearings. The tunnels do not go in straight lines and they are not all on the same level. One thing,' he said, almost laughing, 'if you take a wrong turning you may end up in the pond.'

'Remember,' Commando whispered in my ear, 'if you find yourself going into water, keep your bloody head up. I've done this hundreds of times. If the pipe goes right down into water, take a deep breath and swim like hell. Just keep fucking going. They always come up eventually.'

'Right,' barked Falstaff, 'who's first?'

Cordwell stepped forward. Falstaff murmured to him and opened the drain cover. Cordwell disappeared glumly, down what looked like a ladder. Falstaff pushed the lid just past the vertical position with his foot, and it fell with a deafening clang onto the rim. For five minutes nothing happened.

'Next,' said Falstaff.

Avery stepped forward.

Twenty-five minutes later Cordwell climbed up, covered in sludge, from Scott's drain. After much shouting Scott sent him down again and told him to find the OC: the exit Falstaff had told him to use.

Several more recruits went down at five-minute intervals. Still no one appeared. Brown went next. I was determined to follow him.

I had been caving and pot-holing in my teens so I knew I could do it, but it was not an experience I particularly enjoyed. Once, in the Mendips, a small team of us had to squeeze along a crevice, unable to breathe in deeply due to the confines of space. After about fifty yards the crevice became a tunnel and we inched along it, with our arms squashed against our sides, by propelling ourselves forwards, on our stomachs, with our toes. At one point the tunnel gave way to a fathomless cavern, and we had to cross this darkness to enter the tunnel again. I emerged, slowly, like a worm from its hole, afraid of the emptiness. I forced myself to bridge the cavern, relying on the rigidity of my backbone, until I got my trunk back into the tunnel on the other side of the drop. I was afraid of my body swelling up in the constriction, like an arm in a tourniquet, of being stuck, of being lost underground, and alone.

Falstaff whispered 'OC' in my ear and opened the hatch. I climbed down the steel steps to the wet mud at the bottom. He let the lid fall shut again, and a nauseating echo ran along the dank pipes. I dropped to my hands and knees and started crawling through the sludge, determined that I would count the number of right and left turns. I strained my eyes to see but it was pitch black. The tunnel seemed to curve, very slightly, to the right, but I could not be sure: there was no light.

As I scurried forwards, like a rodent in the dead of night, the water gradually got deeper and I was soon up to my wrists in sediment. I crawled on, chilled and soaking. Had I taken a wrong turning in the darkness? I looked intensely into the distance, like a blind man with open eyes, but could see nothing.

I crawled on and, peering deeper, saw what looked like a thin thread of light. I moved forwards and tried desperately to listen, but I could hear nothing above my own splashes and the slosh of water, as my bulging boots trailed me through the channel. A few yards before the light I put my hand out and it fell on a sodden leg.

'Who the fuck's that?' said a voice, pulling in the limb suddenly.

'Ssh,' I said. 'It's Ballinger.'

'Fucking hell,' the voice said and I recognized it as Avery.

'Are you on your own?' I asked.

'No. Brown's here too.'

I brought one leg forward and knelt on one knee. A trickle of light dripped down the side of Avery's face. 'Is this a junction?' I asked.

'Yes. Where the fuck are you going?'

'The OC,' I whispered, drawing up to Avery and Brown. 'Have you seen anyone else?'

'No. Have you?'

'No. Is this a ventilation shaft?'

'I think so.'

'Where are you going?' I asked Avery.

'The OC.'

'What about you?' I asked the blackness.

'Scott,' came the reply.

'Shit. Where's the OC then?' I said, peering towards Avery.

'How the fuck should I know. I've lost all sense of direction. I'll follow you.'

'I haven't got a clue,' I said. 'First, I thought I was curving to the right, then to the left, and then I went downhill into water.'

'Come on,' said Avery. 'I'll follow you. We can't stay down here all fucking night.'

I squeezed between Avery and Brown, and we moved off again, away from the tiny trace of light, like rats in a disused sewer.

We emerged, eventually, with Cordwell, at the OC. Brown and Commando came out together beneath Scott.

A few people did go missing in the tunnels and had to be hauled out by the instructors. We never saw them again.

At the end of the afternoon Falstaff led us to a commando course. It consisted of a six-foot wall, a rope swing, a bog, a net, a monkey swing and a rope climbing frame. Two laps took seven minutes. We joked afterwards, panting absurdly. Avery said, 'Civilians pay money to do this.' But Commando was disappointed. 'You should try the two-week course we do in the Marines. That'd really test you.'

In the early evening we were stood down until dawn. Scott took the thirty or so of us, as a squadron, off to a small copse on the edge of the training area. The copse was on a steep slope, bordered at the top by a barbed-wire fence and at the bottom by a muddy Land Rover track. The training area itself was the shape of a shallow basin and the sound of small-arms fire, and the slam of car doors, rang out across the depression, as another exercise was being rehearsed somewhere in the distance. We built shelters, called bashas, out of our ponchos by suspending them between the trees with paracord and elastic bungees.

I watched the man next to me. He had twisted his ankle on the commando course and his movements were clumsy. He sat outside his basha with his injured foot stretched out in front of him. He cleared the leaves from a small patch on the ground and cleaned his teeth, spitting out the paste onto the exposed earth. When he had finished he replaced the leaves. Evidence that he had performed this function was concealed from view. He was careful. He was conscious of everything he did. He said a few words and I smiled at him.

I sat quietly in the warmth of the pine needles, with my hexi-stove, watching the sun go down and listening to the birds. As I lay down to rest I thought of all the men around me. How many would survive the course? Would I? A civilian among soldiers, a man with no knowledge of the military among paratroopers who had fought in the Falklands and commandos from Belize.

Five hours later the birds woke me. The sun was shining. I was warm, comfortable and dry. I could see the sky through the trees and to the east the orange glow of the sun rising. I got up slowly, cooked, and packed for parade.

At five o'clock we assembled on the track bordering the woods. Scott found six pieces of litter when we had cleared the site so we began the day with sixty press-ups, ten for each piece. One recruit did not go low enough. '*You!* That's not a fucking press-up. You. Another ten. *Get down.* That's *not* a fucking press-up.' Scott stood on his back so that his chest was forced to the ground. He then grasped the hair on the back of his head and yanked it upwards so that his body was obliged to follow. 'Down.' He stood on his back again. 'Up, down. Up. Down . . .' I looked away. The recruit had been in the regular Pay Corps for eighteen years and had never experienced such aggression. I could see that it disturbed him.

Half an hour later PT began. Two teams had to push a pair of howitzer cannon up and down a hill. A third team, mine, had to pull a Land Rover, with its handbrake on, across country using two enormous lengths of rope with harnesses. As we took up the strain the cord harnesses cut deeply into our shoulders. Defiantly, we bent our backs like slaves to the task, while the OC stood smiling behind his camera tripod, taking photographs for the Training Wing album. Cheops' Pyramid was built like this, I told myself.

Two and a quarter million two-ton limestone blocks. Sweat poured off me. At eight o'clock we stopped and were stood down. It was Sunday.

As we walked back to our bergens I felt relief surge through me. I had survived the first weekend. Sudden activity had dispelled my apprehension. I found my bergen in the middle of the pile and dragged it to one side. I stopped alongside another recruit. He was of medium height and strong. He had come near the front on the eight-mile run, just behind Cordwell. He looked battered and tired, and his dark, unkempt, wavy hair blew in the breeze. He introduced himself as Fowkes.

'Enjoy it?' I asked, trying to start a conversation.

'Yes,' he replied, looking serious. 'An easy start but war won't be like this.' He opened his bergen and pulled out a clean, creased shirt. 'Mind you, no one really wants to fight, except,' he added as an afterthought, 'the Paras: they can't wait.'

WEAPONS

'A dirty soldier,' he was fond of telling his followers, 'means a dirty rifle; and a dirty rifle means, in the long run, a dead soldier.'

Ian Hay

'This,' said Scott, picking up a semi-automatic rifle, 'is the fucking business. You may think you have passed your map-reading, but this is what it's all about.' Scott stared passionately at the rifle: he had retrieved it from the strong-room and held it firmly. 'Just as you would have failed the course,' continued Scott, 'if you'd failed the map-reading test, so we'll bin you if you fail your weapons test.

'From now until Camp, we will practise the drills over and over again. In this regiment they've got to be perfect.

'Forget the TA. This is 21 SAS. If you are nervous people will die. And people have died on Selection. Parachutes are not bigger here. Rounds are not made of rubber. This is fucking real.'

We returned to Cox's Bazar. Hassan said we must buy weapons before going any further. 'If it happens again,' he said, 'they will kill me first, to stop me talking. If I die, you must kill them, sir, before they kill you.'

We looked at the knives for sale in the bazaar, but I knew I could not go on with the trek. I could visualize the consequences if we were confronted again, by a different gang. A crowd squeezing in on me, clubbing me to death, shouting bastard, white monkey

. . . or, perhaps worse, a Third World gaol: a sentence without end.

Back in the barracks, we sat on the floor of the classroom, in a semicircle around our corporal. Each man had one of the new British SA80s resting on his lap. Evening sunlight shone onto, but not through, the small, unwashed window panes. Thick dust had been swept into the skirting boards. A spider scurried up to and around Scott.

'What's this?' Scott held up bits of a firing mechanism. 'You, yes, you on the end. What's your name?'

'Ballinger, staff,' I answered.

'Ballinger, start us off.'

'Um—'

'Come on,' interjected Scott, 'we haven't got all fucking night.'

'I was just thinking, staff.'

'Thinking!' ejected Scott. 'Thinking . . . Jesus Christ. The man next to you. Yes, you. Start us off. Thinking,' muttered Scott under his breath, 'thinking.'

The man next to me ran through the parts effortlessly, slipping up only at the flash eliminator.

'Did you get that, Ballinger?' said Scott.

'Yes, staff,' I said, foolishly exposing myself, for I had retained less than two-thirds of what my neighbour had said.

To my relief, however, Scott, in a rare display of generosity, replied, 'Don't worry, Ballinger, we'll deal with you later.'

At the end of the session Scott asked if there were any questions. I hesitated before asking, 'How does it work?'

'How does what work, Ballinger?'

'The rifle,' I replied. Suddenly all eyes turned on me.

'The what, Ballinger?'

'The rifle, staff.' The heads turned away and looked again at Scott.

'*The weapon, Ballinger.* We call it a weapon, not a fucking rifle. Remember that. Nothing upsets me more than to hear some waster calling it a fucking rifle. Don't worry how it works. We'll cover that in another lesson.'

As we filed down the stairs to the strong-room, Avery came up to me smiling. 'Fancy asking Scott how it works. I bet he doesn't even know.'

I laughed. 'I was just curious.'

Avery looked at me quizzically. 'Were you in the Paras?'

'No.'

'Funny,' he said, 'I could have sworn you were until this evening.'

When the Storeman arrived he unlocked the large reinforced door and swung it back on its steel hinges. He let us walk inside for the first time. Racks, against all four walls, stretched from floor to ceiling. Each one contained something different, and the guns, like books in a library, had been organized according to type and series. Some of the bigger pieces of equipment lay horizontally, like bottles in a cellar. Others had been stacked vertically.

Avery was agape at what he saw. 'Jesus,' he said, walking over to a rack of black tubes that looked like a set of modified drain pipes. 'Where did you get these?'

'Customs and Excise,' the Storeman replied. 'Most of the weapons in here have been seized. The AK47s came from the Middle East. Those came from Belgium . . . Blokes in the regular army will never even see weapons like this. You lot don't know you're born. You'll be practising with all of these before you're through.'

Avery grinned, like a small boy who walks into a toy shop for the first time. 'Even the Gun Club doesn't have this variety,' he said, turning to me.

'Gun Club?'

'Yes. I shoot most lunchtimes.'

While changing for PT, I overheard a conversation between Fowkes and another recruit. He was a small, lean man with cropped blond hair. Two or three tattoos were visible on each arm.

'I was in the Paras, too,' was the first thing I heard Fowkes say. 'Were you in 2 Para?'

'Yes,' came the reply.

'Did you go to the Falklands?' Fowkes asked, undressing at the same time.

'Yes.'

'What was it like?'

'Fucking loved it. That's why I'm here.'

No one spoke, and then Fowkes continued.

'Did you kill anyone?'

'Shut up, Fowkes,' said Cordwell.

'Saddest thing I saw,' said the Para, 'was one bloke: 'alf his head had gone.'

A MOUNTAIN SHUFFLE

Tut, never fear me: I am vigilant as a cat to steal cream.

Shakespeare

Two weeks after our first weekend, I stood with the other recruits in a lonely lay-by in North Wales. We were queuing up at the tail-gate of a four-ton truck for two twenty-four-hour ration packs each. Not long after the last man had collected his supplies the Storeman switched off the generator and it was quiet once more. The stars shone brightly but it was pitch black in the pine woods where we were sleeping.

I crawled into my sleeping bag and for a while lay quite still. One or two others were fumbling with their rations in the darkness, but, unable to see a thing, they too soon gave up. There was no wind and the woods were silent.

I woke, with the rustle of recruits, at six o'clock. I crawled through the pine needles, dragging my kit with me, and tidied my bergen on the tarmac of the lay-by. The sun shone and I longed to be off, climbing in the cool of the early morning, and striding across the hills against a fabulous backdrop of green pasture, and an intense and constant blue sky.

Scott appeared and told us to form up in three ranks for inspection. For two hours, as the sun rose, we stood on the edge of the woods showing the contents of our bergens to the inspecting corporals. One recruit had forgotten to bring a pen, another a notebook, another a compass; the list went on and on. Every omission caused a problem, and if a man had forgotten something, Falstaff, who was springing around on the verge, made a note of his name in a little book.

'You are a marked man, Fowkes,' said Scott, realizing that Fowkes had forgotten to buy a spare pair of batteries for his torch.

'Listen in, lads,' the OC said, when the inspection was finally over. 'The aim of this exercise is to give all recruits practical experience in navigation on the hills, with a bergen on, in the hours of daylight and darkness. For the duration of this exercise you will walk, with your corporals, in squadrons. Any questions?'

We walked all morning and all afternoon with frequent spells of running and sprinting. Occasionally we stopped to assess our position and ostensibly to practise taking compass bearings. At one such stop the little Commando sat on his bergen next to me. When Scott had finished pointing out the features on the ground, and we had, thereby, pinpointed our position on the map, Commando leant across to me and said, 'How do you take a bearing from the map?'

I was just showing him, discreetly, lest Scott should see us whispering, when Falstaff suddenly wafted, like a jinnee, out of the trees.

'Listen to your corporal,' he said, scowling at me, as if something unpleasant had just woken him up. 'Every time you stop, your senses should be tingling. Study your map. Check your position and then re-check it.'

Everyone stopped what they were doing, but no one turned around to look. Even Scott kept quiet.

'Think you know all this, do you?'

'No, sir.'

'Think you don't have to listen, do you?'

'No, sir.'

'Well, fucking well listen then. When your corporal's talking, you shut up. One hundred per cent attention. Is that clear?'

'Yes, sir.'

'Listen then. I'll be watching you.'

At the end of the march we were stood down for four hours. I put up a double basha with Commando on a steep slope in some pine woods. Not far away, sparkling water slid over a series of falls into a run of small, deep plunge-pools.

'How's your knee?' I asked Commando, as we sat cooking some of our rations.

'It's all right. Don't worry about me. I'll be doing some circuit training when we get back to barracks.'

'I should rest it if I were you. You've only got two weeks until the next exercise.'

'I'll be all fucking right.'

'Have any of your family been in the army?' I asked, pushing two tins of bacon burgers around a mess tin of boiling water.

'Yes. They all have. My father was in the Commandos during the war. His father was in the Royal Welch Fusiliers, so was Uncle Roddy. Uncle George—'

'Why did you leave the Marines then?'

'I'd had enough. Went to the Sudan for three months. I was trained in Supplies. Unbelievable. I'd never seen so much suffering.'

For almost an hour I rested in the shade of our double basha. The sun trickled down to us through the trees and, as the afternoon began to slide gently into evening, the temperature dropped quickly.

Our huge, square sail flaps and billows in the wind. We pass among wooden boats, laden almost to sinking with roughly crafted bricks. Buzzards fly in tight circles around the mast of our boat. A coxswain sits alone under a faded umbrella, out of the burning sun.

Hassan and I sit towards the stern. I squat in silence and watch the changing scenes on the river bank. Hassan is smoking, peacefully, in the empty hull. We are a strange crew: three or four deck hands, the coxswain, Hassan and I, and a couple of boys.

Hassan says we will stop, somewhere south of Dhaka, to pick up some bricks. We will drop them off again on our way to Barisal.

One of the boys is standing on the side of the boat, urinating into

the water. The other boy, who is alongside him, is collecting
drinking water in a rusty tin that once contained evaporated milk.
He has just dropped the sharp-edged tin, on a string, into the water.
Now, he is pulling the sloshing liquid aboard to quench his thirst.

We stop against a muddy embankment, below a brick factory.
A row of planks is thrown rapidly down, across the marshy ground,
and up onto the side of our boat. Boys and girls are walking down
them quickly, towards us, with baskets of bricks on their heads,
struggling to retain their balance. They drop their loads into the
hold. They return carrying their empty receptacles, the way they
have come, competing for space on the narrow planks. Some
children carry their burdens loosely, with no basket, on their heads.
A small handkerchief pad spreads the weight. An older man sits,
higher up the incline, under a canopy, on a wooden chair that has
partially sunk into the wet clay. He is probably the paymaster. He
is watching the operation, but says little. The children know what
to do.

Further downstream some laundry has been left on the reeds to
dry in the sun. Nearby, the washing is still in progress. I can hear
the clap across the water as wet, twisted lungis are thrashed against
the smooth, flat stones.

We sail on, all day and all night. At dawn the next day, we stop
again. A flat jute field stretches endlessly in all directions. There are
not many trees now and those that stand do so alone. All but one
or two of the coconuts have been picked. Hassan has gone off to
find another boat. Our current boatman will go no further: he is
afraid to go beyond the territory he knows. I settle down on an
upturned plastic crate, and wait.

It is early and silent. Small wooden boats lie in the still, mercurial
waters. Each one has a canopy of reeds, woven and bent in a
semicircle over the middle of the craft, so that all but the bow and
the stern are in shade. There is no current here, and the little boats
lie motionless in the sheltered bay. Dawn reflections shimmer in
the warm waters.

Hassan returns with a fat, dishevelled man who leads us to
another boat, a small motor launch that will take us, eventually, to

Barguna. We clamber onto its metal deck. There is room, perhaps, for twenty people, but there is no shade. Hassan says there will be at least seventeen stops before we arrive. We sit quietly on the warm metal, worn smooth by countless human feet.

The port begins to stir. A few more passengers arrive. A weak, hungry man, with a stomach bloated to a hideous size, is helped aboard. Hassan says there has been a religious festival, not far away, and this man has travelled, like many others, for a day and a night, to be present for the distribution of bread. He sits with his legs crossed, his dry back arched to the sun, and his belly hiding his feet. A little boy is sitting next to him and the old man keeps touching his head, endearingly, with his weak hand.

The captain arrives and a few minutes later we chug noisily out into the current. For hours progress is painstakingly slow, and we stop often. At last we moor again, against another muddy embankment at the end of a rice paddy. A grey-haired Bengali has just come aboard. When he notices me he adjusts his black plastic glasses, held together with sticky tape, and says, simply, 'Cambridge?'

The sun has risen high in the sky and is beating down relentlessly on the metal deck. The temperature of the steel plates has risen and I can feel the heat through the soles of my shoes. I sit on my small bag of belongings, my skin blistering but not burning in the heat. My throat is rough and dry: it is difficult to talk. I shiver uncomfortably.

'You know, the British built some of these bridges,' he says, pointing vaguely into the distance. I try to follow his gesture but can see nothing. It is too hot to move.

'I know Shakespeare. Very great Englishman,' he continues. 'Listen,' he says, and he recites some lines in broken English. '*Tempest*. You know Shakespeare?'

The captain pulls a string in his cabin and a bell rings in the tiny engine-room below. The invisible mechanic puts the engine into gear, and we move off, slowly, away from the littered river bank.

Sticky Tape introduces himself as the local schoolteacher. At this, even Hassan looks up. He asks about the Queen and he wants me to sing our National Anthem. I sing the first verse, quietly. Even the poor man with the distended belly turns to watch. Eyes full of suffering and sorrow stare at me across the cramped deck.

Sticky Tape has started singing. 'This is Bengali Anthem,' he says, interrupting himself. He sings with a menacing wail, and through broken teeth. Beads of sweat cling to his forehead and glisten in the sun. Tears fill his eyes and run down his sunken cheek bones, all too visible through his sallow skin. A few children clap. But now there is silence again. Mostly the children lie asleep, curled up in the tiny patch of shadow created by the frail bodies of their parents. It is too hot to entertain, and too hot to listen to another man's song.

Around eight o'clock, Commando, who had snored continuously for the last hour, suddenly woke up and began to pack away his kit. Since my tranquillity was disturbed, I did likewise. At eight-thirty, in semi-darkness and somewhat casually, we stood on parade.

The OC went berserk. 'You lot are too fucking sloppy. It's going to be as black as a witch's tit up there.' He nodded in the direction of the hills. The sun had set and visibility was decreasing rapidly. 'I don't want to see any stragglers. You've got to sharpen up, lads.'

By the early hours of the morning we had still not made our final rendezvous (RV). The last three miles were a haul, for I was blessed with juicy blood blisters on the balls of both feet. The terrain had been hard going: clumpy grass for seven hours. Eventually the end came, and I fell asleep in my basha shortly before dawn.

An hour later someone kicked me in the ribs. I was on watch. I got up and the insects were terrible. Fowkes was wide awake. He had not slept at all. A fly had got stuck in his ear and buzzed around frantically, trying, without success, to find the exit. He had spent the last hour slapping the side of his head instead of sleeping.

'I nearly had a sense of humour failure,' he said, when he saw me pacing around between the trees.

Everyone had to be ready for PT at seven o'clock. I had been up since five but was too tired to be really efficient. I woke up, forty minutes later, half-way to the thirtieth press-up.

'Come on, lads, one more for the Paras . . . One more for the Gay Boys . . . One for the Wimps. *Come on*, push it. Drive it out. OK. Good effort. Fall in. *Move!* We are going to run back to the basha area. I don't want to see any stragglers. Got it?'

We ran to fall in, in three ranks behind the OC, like school-children lined up behind their form mistress on an outing. The OC paced us for several miles around the quiet lanes, until we came back to our campsite.

Fowkes and I came in in the upper quartile. The OC was furious with the stragglers. Commando was one of the last men in. 'You blokes are deluding yourselves . . . This is the fucking kindergarten stage . . . An easy mountain shuffle . . . Some of you are fucking hopeless . . . This is *not* the fucking Girl Guides . . . You have got to dig in . . . It's a mental attitude . . . You must exercise in fifties: fifty press-ups, fifty sit-ups . . . Gone are the days of tens . . . Some of you blokes are no fucking hopers. Wasters. Bloody wasters.'

GIN AND TONIC

It is not good to be too free.
It is not good to have all one needs.

Pascal

'More torture,' said Fowkes. At his feet, his bergen and all his kit was laid out, almost randomly, for inspection. 'Mind you,' continued Fowkes in his slightly Scottish accent, 'you can't beat a good dose of misery. It teaches you to appreciate the important things in life.' We were back at the barracks among a pile of equipment, waiting for the OC to arrive and give us a set of orders for the next weekend.

'I hate this bit,' said Brown, turning to join us. 'It's the hanging around. Anything is better than waiting.'

Another recruit, wearing an Everest T-shirt, asked me if I thought I would survive the course. I laughed. 'I've no idea. Do you think you will?'

'No,' he said. 'Scott had me nearly delirious last weekend. I'm just doing it to see how far I can get. That's the same with most of the blokes here.'

'Where's Commando, then?' inquired Brown, looking at me.

'I don't know. He said he'd be here. He skipped PT on the drill night because of his knee. He's probably still injured.'

'What's wrong with it?'

'He said he had an operation in the Marines, and the military doctor botched it up.'

'You don't believe that, do you?'

'Why not? It's what he said.'

'There's nothing wrong with him. He's putting it on.'

Avery, who was standing beside us, said, 'He won't turn up. He's frightened of failing.'

'All set?' said Scott, walking over to the five of us, in his civilian clothes.

'Where's Commando?' asked Fowkes.

'He's not coming,' said Scott, squinting. 'You won't see him again. Don't worry, you won't even remember his name in a year's time.'

'Listen in, lads,' the OC said, striding boldly, and informally, out onto the parade-ground. 'Met: first light, 03.25; last light, 21.46; moon, one-quarter full. Forecast: stormy with mist on the hills. Humidity: ninety-six per cent. Temperature on the tops: eighty-one degrees. Basically, lads, it's going to be hot and sticky. Bloody hot.

'Aim: to build up stamina by carrying a forty-pound bergen over arduous terrain during the hours of daylight and darkness.'

We loaded the vehicles and set off for another unknown destination.

At one o'clock in the morning the mist hung low and it was raining hard. I climbed a barbed-wire fence in the dark and found a depression in some long wet grass. I made a crude basha, which was a grave error. Within minutes I was drenched. Soggy, tired and cold, I got up at five o'clock.

That day, we walked, climbed and ran in our squadrons for nine hours without a break. We rarely used paths and never roads. We went from A to B, usually on a compass bearing. At the end, high up in the hills of North Wales, Scott stopped us and each man sat on his bergen, grateful for the rest. We sat in a curve, two or three rows deep, around him. The wind whistled over the ridge, and our smocks, soaked with sweat, flapped against our skin.

Scott explained the RV drills. On the next weekend we would walk in pairs, and after that alone. At each RV we would be given a new grid reference and told to run to it as fast as possible. They might be separated by two miles or twenty. We would not know until we were given the grid reference. The RV might be one of five or one of fifteen. One thing was sure, Scott said, we would never know in advance how far the march was. We would never know how long we had, and we would never know where the end was, until we got there. 'Always expect more,' he kept saying. 'But don't save yourselves. It's one hundred per cent all the time. You go absolutely flat out.'

Each RV would be manned, and we would have to approach each one, running, looking determined and smart, with a clear head, and prepared to answer any questions put to us. In particular, we must be wearing our cap-comforters, whatever the weather, have all our buttons done up, and the map available for questions. We must not, on any account, write anything down. All grid references, at each RV, would be given twice only, and would have to be memorized.

'By the end of the day, you may have twenty or more six-figure numbers to remember, so concentrate,' said Scott. 'It's not easy when you've run twenty miles with a forty-pound bergen. Don't switch off.'

When he had finished talking, he told us to line up behind a large boulder a hundred yards down the wet mountainside. Each man was to run up to him at full speed and shout out his name, number and squadron, as if Scott was the corporal at an RV. Three-quarters of the recruits had already gone through the routine when my turn came. I bolted up the slope and shouted into the wind, in between heaving gasps. Scott stopped me before I had finished.

'You, Ballinger,' he said, screwing up his dark eyes, 'have got to be a lot more aggressive. Let him know where you've come from. Let him know you mean business. Be more aggressive, Ballinger. You're too fucking casual. Get back down there, and do it again. *Switch on.*' He pointed to the boulder and I ran back down to it.

For two hours in Barisal I stood on deck and watched huge hessian sacks of rice being dropped into the steel hull. Down below, in infernal heat, men in soiled lungis, slippery with sweat, struggled to unhook the cargo from the dockside crane. Onshore, a bespectacled old man sat underneath a lone light bulb in a corrugated iron warehouse. Painstakingly, he logged each sack of rice onto the boat.

Our cabin was grimy, as hot and humid as a steel greenhouse. At the far end was a metal cubicle with a door like a submarine hatch. Inside was a stained lavatory which stank of stale urine. A yellow, ribbed metal plate had been bolted on top of the Western-style porcelain basin. In the middle of this was a hole the size of a man's fist. You had to step up onto the metal plate, squat and hope for a good aim. The water, which was a horrible brown, spurted inconsistently from a single tap. There was no basin. The tap was screwed to the steel partition, six inches from the floor. It could not be turned. The screw had jammed and water gurgled onto the floor of its own accord. In the cabin itself a fan sat on top of a wooden cupboard. I followed the wire. It led to a loose socket and the bare ends had been forced into it with sticks. I switched it on. The fan rotated with a good velocity but it had only one blade, which was broken. We had bunks, each with a thin, brown, synthetic mattress.

We started off in our cabin and then, when it became unbearable, and the sticky heat too intense, went outside to sleep on deck. About midnight, Hassan, shivering with jaundice, went back to his bunk. I did not sleep well and got up at dawn to explore the boat.

It was a small cargo ship built in Hamburg, probably designed for between fifty and a hundred people. There were about a thousand people on board, and Hassan and I calculated, on the basis of fifty chickens per cage, a further two thousand squawking birds. All day we sat among them. Some kept blinking, covering their eyes with their wrinkled, pink eyelids to prevent them from dehydrating completely.

In the afternoon, not a yard away, a fight broke out. A dense crowd surrounded two men. A small man started clubbing a much larger man about the head with a cruel stick, until his filthy grey singlet was splattered with blood. Doubled up with pain, he cast his vest overboard. In the crush I caught glimpses: a torn ear, a smashed face, a laceration, loose skin. Terror. The big man collapsed onto the deck, blood running from his head. I pushed my way back through the crowd and found Hassan, but when I told him he did not even sigh. He knew too well what had happened.

'Thief, sir.'

A tiny brown Bengali, naked, except for a rag around his privates, pushed past me brandishing a rusty knife and grinning hideously.

Someone cut the big man's hands off. Hassan told me later that he had been pushed over the side.

The captain, unaware of what had happened, stopped the boat for two hours. We had to wait, during the heat of the day, for the tide to rise to avoid getting stuck on a sandbank. A middle-aged man left his family and washed the blood off the deck with a bucket of water. The wooden planks dried quickly in the sun.

At dusk I went back to our cabin to try to sleep. At first it was just about possible by ignoring the stench and the cockroaches, but I awoke to tears. Hassan was crying. I spoke to him a couple of times but there was no response. I put on my shoes and sat in the corner. He continued to cry. A little later he got up and we talked about his circumstances. He so much wanted to come travelling with me and then he was struck down with jaundice.

'Always work, sir. Every day work. Else death,' he said, in between his choking tears.

He hated the boat and his temper ran short. I was frightened. We were on an overcrowded boat and the atmosphere was still charged. He was crying mostly over his parents, and over his life, which he saw as a gross injustice. I was keen to get out of the confines of the cabin in case he lost control of himself. I opened the door, and eventually we went out onto the top deck.

It was a starry night. We leant on the rail of the boat in silence for some time. The tension cooled in the clear air.

'Do you like the stars?'

'Yes,' he said.

'What do you think?' I asked.

'Stars are always shining and smiling.'

'What do you think they are?'

'Very Holy, sir. Very Holy.'

'Do they make you feel small?'

'Yes, sir, very small. Like a tiny stone.'

We looked out to sea, the Bay of Bengal. The rippling waves reflected the lights of passing boats. Hassan asked me about the seas and rivers in England. 'You can see to the bottom of some rivers,' I said, leaning over the rail. I realized straight away that I had offended him. He became very defensive about the Bay. It was clean enough, he said, for him to drink, but not for me.

As we leant on the railings, in the moonlight, Hassan said, 'One day, sir, you will buy a boat. You will be the captain and pull the string. I will work the engine and collect the money. Seventy-five per cent for you, twenty-five for me.'

I laughed out loud and said, 'No. Fifty, fifty.'

The corners of his eyes filled with tears. 'Thank you, sir.'

When we stopped at the end of the afternoon, wet with sweat and with aching shoulders, we literally fell down. The rain had stopped and before long every man had stripped to the waist to cool off and expose his sores.

Bashas went up slowly. Slowly, because we were exhausted. The command, 'No move before 21.00', had been given so we had an abundance of time. Tumbling, grey clouds passed rapidly overhead, leaving, like a quick scene change, a brilliant blue sky.

Just as we were attending to our injuries, Scott and the Sergeant-Major began a lackadaisical inspection of our bashas. They were hysterically funny, more like sun awnings than bashas. The man next to me sat, quite happily, under the middle of his. He was a powerful man, just under six feet tall. He had taken off his smock and he sat in a singlet, with the name of a university rowing club embossed on the front. Each corner of his rectangular poncho had been tied, at the same height, about four feet above the ground, to four perfectly spaced trees. The middle had been pulled upwards, with an elasticated bungee, and fastened to an overhanging branch.

From the side it looked like an old-fashioned Chinaman's hat.

'What the hell do you call this?' the Sergeant-Major asked, bending down to look at the man inside.

'It's my basha, staff,' he answered, proudly.

'A basha? You look as though you should be serving gin and tonics. What's your name?'

'White, sir,' he said smiling, his face streaked with sweat and dirt.

Minutes before the night march began the Sergeant-Major conducted a more formal inspection. To my relief he passed me without comment but stopped dead at White who was standing next to me. White had put all of his rubbish into an old plastic bag.

'Harrods!' he spluttered, visibly shocked, but then his countenance changed. 'One Squadron are you?'

'Yes, sir,' said White, springing to attention.

'Thought so.'

When the Sergeant-Major was out of earshot White turned to me and whispered, 'What's he worried about, it's green isn't it?'

A DRILL NIGHT

To have a strong character one must have experienced the effect produced by others upon oneself: therefore others are a necessity.

Stendhal

'OK, Cordwell, you've been in the army before, perhaps you'd like to explain the different types of wind.'

Cordwell stood up, proudly, at the front of the classroom, kicking a leg of his desk as he did so, and turned to face us. The crumples in his shirt were just visible in the dim light, but surprisingly the Sergeant-Major had not noticed this during our brief parade. It was a wet, blustery evening and the OC had come out and cut short the inspection. We went to our lessons five minutes early.

'There are three types of wind, in the army,' said Cordwell, grinning at us.

As he spoke, the classroom door shook in the draught and the canopy of corrugated iron rattled in the rain.

'Jesus Christ,' exclaimed Scott. 'You're full of fucking wind.'

When the laughter had died down, Cordwell took a deep breath, his small chest filled out, and he continued. 'There is no wind, fresh wind and strong wind. When there is no wind, the range flag hangs vertically. And when there is a fresh wind,' said Cordwell, warming to his subject, 'it is half out, like a droopy knob. And when there is a strong wind, it is completely horizontal.'

At this, the rows of recruits collapsed into sobs of laughter. It was some time before Scott got the lesson back on course and explained that, when taking aimed shots at distances of greater than one hundred metres, one had to take account of the direction and strength of the wind. He also talked us through the principles of marksmanship and the different methods of engaging targets.

After our lesson was over we walked across the parade-ground to the changing rooms and dressed for PT. Scott had decided to vary our routine and, from now until Camp, he said we would do interval training. This consisted of twelve four-hundred-metre sprints. Each one had to be run in less than seventy seconds and there was a sixty-second rest between each lap.

No one ever enjoyed this routine, and frequently a man was sick. One week, when we had recovered from this sequence, Avery turned to Brown and me and said, 'Do either of you fancy a drink?'

'Where?' I asked.

'Brown and I know a quiet place. It's not far.'

Brown looked at his watch. 'It will have to be a quick one.'

We climbed into Avery's Golf and drove to a small pub.

'What do you think of Scott, then?' I asked, when all three of us were sitting down.

'He's twisted.' Brown leant back on his stool. 'He's unbalanced. He puts me off, actually. I hope not all the men in the regiment are like him.'

'He's got it in for you, Avery,' I said.

'I know, that's what worries me.'

'Keep your head down, and you'll be all right,' said Brown.

'Did you two know each other before you met in the TA?' I asked.

'Yes. We were at Oxford together,' said Brown.

'Were you? Which Colleges?'

'Avery was at Univ and I was at Queens.'

'Same year?'

'Yes.'

'I read Physics,' said Avery. 'Brown read PPE.'

'Did you know Cordwell at Oxford?'

'No. He read Maths at Cambridge. We met him later in the TA. Brown says you went to Oxford.'

'Yes. A year before you, though.'

'You know,' said Avery, looking around the almost deserted bar, and lowering his voice, 'the reason the SAS badge is a mixture of light and dark blue is because there were so many Oxbridge graduates in the original regiment.'

When we had finished our drinks, Brown climbed into the back of Avery's car and I got into the front passenger seat. 'Are you enjoying the course, Avery?' I asked.

'I wouldn't say I was enjoying it, exactly,' he said, pulling out into the traffic, 'but it does give you a chance of distinguishing yourself, physically.'

'But don't you find it difficult trying to work in a bank and do this, what with training every evening? I always seem to be shattered.'

'This is more important than my job.' Avery sounded emphatic. 'After all, how many merchant banks are there? And how many SAS regiments could I join? . . . Just the one, actually. I can't see myself being able to do this at any other stage of my life. Besides,' he added, after a pause, 'Selection has totally changed my outlook on life.'

'What, already? In what way?'

Brown, leaning forward, with his elbows resting on the backs of our seats, was also interested in Avery's reply.

'Bullshit,' he said. 'I can't take bullshit any more. Also I am much more aggressive.'

COMEDY

Rivers are moving roads which take us where we want to go.

Pascal

Forty kilometres of countryside lay before us. This was a race in pairs. White looked at me and said, 'We'll win this one.'

The OC made a note of the time, and, like the man with the starter gun on a school sports day, fired a blank. Thirty or forty pairs ran forwards and White and I were off with a dash.

The moment we started my stomach settled. White, an ox of a man, like me sweated without restraint and sweat we did. It was 100° Fahrenheit and we wore smocks and cap-comforters, and carried heavy bergens.

Together, we launched ourselves aggressively into the countryside before us. We were the first pair to the first, second and third RVs. The next stretch was a very long one and, before we were half-way along it, we were forced to make a detour for water. Consequently, we lost valuable time and slipped to third place. Soon, after what we guessed to be the penultimate RV, White began to lose consciousness: his head kept swaying and he started to stumble. I insisted we lose height quickly; water was our top priority. White said nothing but instantly disappeared over the edge of the mountain. I followed, thrashing my way through waist-deep bracken and dense heather, struggling like a fly ensnared in a spider's web.

'Steady on, White,' I gasped, catching up with him and disen-tangling myself from lengths of briar and undergrowth. 'This is stupid.' I was sweating more than ever. We struck a tributary at a point where a half-decomposed sheep lay across a waterfall, and drank upstream. Our final RV was a bridge at the end of the next valley. 'Can you make it?' I asked White, without looking at him, but there was no answer. I turned. His eyes were rolling. He was in a daze, on the point of collapse. '*White!*'

'You lead,' he said, unsteady on his feet.

We descended the valley and struggled up the other side. Once on the ridge we could see the RV more clearly. An ambling track high up on the hillside arrived there eventually, but the route was long and well above the river.

'I've got to get down to water,' said White.

Again we plunged down another steep valley through dense thistles and over barbed-wire fences until we hit the river. White staggered into the water up to his knees and fell down.

'Jesus Christ, I needed that,' he said, as he lifted his head out of the water.

I stood on the bank and looked at him. The water held an attraction. We revised our plan and agreed to follow the river bank down to the final RV. There was a path, not marked on the map, that looked promising. We walked along it until it ran straight into the fast-flowing river, and then stopped.

Slabs of rock soared, straight upwards, out of the water. Trees thick with moss hung low overhead, excluding most of the sunlight but none of the heat. Where there was no rock the foliage was so dense as to be impenetrable.

'Let's go down the river,' said White. 'It's bound to go to the bridge.' We had few options.

We waded uneasily up to our thighs. The rocks on the bottom were slippery and slimy. Hot, sticky and desperate, we stumbled noisily downstream.

'White, this is madness,' I said. 'Thank God no one can see us now.'

Drenched to the skin, we climbed one otters' dam after another.

It took us an hour to cover a kilometre.

At last the path left the river. It climbed steeply and somewhat uncertainly. We took it, but before we were one hundred feet above the water, it was slashed by a barbed-wire fence. White beat me there and quickly flung his bergen from his shoulders, up against a tree on the far side of the fence. He put one foot on the wire and then, for a fraction of a second, stood still, glued in position, like a child at a zoo who suddenly sees a sleeping lion move. Momentarily transfixed, we watched his unstable bergen topple sideways and trip over the roots of the tree. It tumbled, twisted, picked up speed, bounced and finally plunged, like a dislodged boulder, into the river far below where it was seized by the current and moved gracefully out into the flow. Before the same second was over I saw, in my mind's eye, White's bergen floating peacefully into the RV without him, but before I could say anything he came to his senses, leapt the fence, threw himself down the slope and literally fell into the river. The marvel is that he landed on his feet and did not fall over. With the water running around his waist, he dived on his bergen as if it was the deciding tackle in a rugby match.

The path led us to the final RV and we came in tenth.

The last RV was a small humpbacked bridge spanning the river. On one side of the water, the rock rose vertically and tall trees grew in deep fissures. On the other side, just before the bridge, there was a grass clearing. It was large enough to accommodate several four-ton trucks, before the trees began again. A wire boundary fence ran along the top of the bank, between the river and the patch of pasture.

I built a lean-to basha against the fence, at the end of a line of shelters already there. White built his alongside. Leaving my kit in the shade, I took the aluminium canteen from my webbing, climbed the fence and stepped down to the river. Within seconds I was sitting naked and up to my chest in a deep pool. Dousing myself with the canteen, I splashed and wallowed in the cold depths like a baby chuckling in a bath. Moments later, half a dozen others had joined me. The sun shone through the trees and the water sparkled innocently as it slipped and gurgled around our sore bodies. Like raucous holiday-makers in a swimming pool, swapping stories and telling of their antics the night before, we too joked about our errors, our successes, our routes and, most importantly, our injuries. As time wore on, one by one we walked back to our bashas. I laid my clothes, soaked with sweat and river water, out in the sun to dry.

Sitting outside my basha, with my socks off, feeling the breeze blow between my toes, I was struck by the composition of our small campsite. There were dozens of lean-to bashas in a row; men, stripped to the waist, tired, hungry and thirsty; men with blood-stained feet, blistered and bruised, each applying his own medication, or queuing up to see the medic, depending on his inclination or tolerance of pain.

White's bergen had rubbed the superficial skin off his spine and the scar stung when he lay back in the grass.

He propped himself up on his elbow, and said, wincing, 'I could have been sailing this weekend with my girlfriend, in Poole Harbour.'

'I bet you wish you were, now. I was on Lundy Island last week with mine. The weather was perfect. I spent the whole holiday running up and down cliffs, and sprinting around the island, trying to get fit. It seems so stupid now.'

'I don't do that much,' he said, sitting up. 'I find I can get by with one major run a week. I play rugby in between and that helps. I just haven't got the time for more than that.'

'What does your girlfriend think of the TA?' I asked.

'She doesn't like it at all. We're both doctors and she is on call one weekend in three. If I do this one weekend, and she's on call the next, and I'm back here again the following weekend, we might not see each other for three or four weeks. It's hopeless.'

'Have you told her what you're doing?'

'No. She just thinks it's the TA. She thinks we sit in a ditch all weekend and eat crab sandwiches. Have you told yours?'

'No. I haven't told anyone. I'm not going to.'

As we sat talking, a cloud, that had been concealing the sun,

slipped through the sky, and our bodies once again cast long
shadows across the grass. Every so often, a four-ton truck would
drive up the tyred track in the woods and stop outside the OC's
tent. It came laden with recruits, men Falstaff had retrieved from
the hills, suffering from heat stroke, dehydration or exhaustion.
Their final pain was to line up outside the OC's tent, and be told,
confidentially and one at a time, that they had failed the course.

Of about sixty-nine runners, thirty-two saw the medic. Six were
diagnosed as serious.

At nine o'clock in the evening the night march began and lasted
most of the night. At first light we assembled for PT.

After fifteen minutes, when we dropped down into the press-up
position, Avery, solid with cramp, collapsed onto the gravel. Scott
noticed, and, shamed that a man in his squadron was unable to
punch out fifty press-ups, dragged him to the front of the car-park.
There, in front of us all, he made him push out press-up after press-
up. When Avery had finished, we formed up in squadrons.

'I could feel that,' I murmured to him. 'I couldn't bear to look.'

'I had my eyes closed too,' he said, looking straight ahead.

'OK, lads,' the OC said, when he had paced us back to the basha
area. 'Some of you put in a good effort. Well done, but this is not
a hill walking club. On the next exercise, we really crank it up. I
don't want to see anyone limping. If you get blisters, so fucking
what. It's only fucking pain. Remember, lads, a day is but twenty-
four hours long.'

OPERA

'Listen in, lads. This weekend is the first time you walk alone. Bergens will weigh fifty-five pounds. I shall be checking them on the hills, so don't think you can put a rock in them, just before the RV. If I catch any man under weight, he's straight off the course. No one carries less than fifty-five pounds.'

When the OC had concluded his brief, we loaded our kit onto the back of the squadron four-tonner, climbed aboard, and stretched out on the ribbed metal floor. There were about twenty of us, jumbled up with a bergen and a kit bag each. We coughed our way out of the barracks on yet another Friday evening. The exhaust fumes, for some reason, were always sucked into the back. Eventually, we got up to our top speed of fifty miles per hour with the roof and top-sides, which were made of canvas, flapping noisily in the wind. This continued until we reached our destination in North Wales some time during the night.

I woke up, having slept poorly, beneath a dawn sky softened with sinewy, white clouds. I was anxious and tired.

Scott addressed us as a squadron. 'Right, I want to see you fucking move this weekend. Piss on the other squadrons. I expect you lot to come in first. Is that understood? OK. Fall in with the others for the OC's orders.'

We joined the other recruits for the start of yet another exercise. We totalled fifty-eight in number, and about twenty of these came from One Squadron.

'Listen, lads,' the OC began, looking towards the mountains. 'The streams are empty up there. Make sure both your water-bottles are full. Carry extra in your bergens if you can. If any man needs more water go and fill up now, from the jerry cans.'

A few recruits fell out, ran to the Storeman's four-tonner, and boosted their water supplies. When they came back the OC continued.

'This, lads, is a race. I don't want to see anyone bimbling around the hills. I shall be watching you,' he said, brandishing a high-powered telescope. 'One tip, lads: don't stop. Just keep fucking going. When I dismiss you, line up in front of the PSI. He will start you off.'

We stood, stretching out in a long line from Falstaff, at the bottom of a mountain, just as schoolboys stand together at the start of a hundred-yard sprint. There was no stagger in this race: no allowance was made for the weak. It was man against man, and each man against himself. We all carried identical loads. Our weapons weighed the same and only a fool did not carry as much water as he could. I adjusted my cap-comforter and pursed my dry lips in anticipation of the start. I was desperate to get moving, to get it over with.

A gun fired: we were off.

The mountainside was soon crawling with men, but I climbed in solitude. Few people spoke. The sun beat down on the scree slopes and we stumbled slowly upwards. High above us, Scott sat manning the RV on the summit. Eventually I made it up to him and shouted out my name, number and squadron, dispassionately and cruelly. Satisfied with my façade of aggression, he gave me the next RV. It was at the bottom again.

I jolted down the jagged scree slope, my bergen bouncing up and down on my back, purposefully and aggressively, lest the OC had me in his telescopic sights. Falstaff was at the RV and he sent me up again, by a different route.

At the top, I gave Scott the same details in a hard, hollow voice. He seemed pleased. The next RV was a barn, some miles away, at sea level.

I ran over the ridge and, when out of sight of Scott, pulled off my cap-comforter. Bending under the burden of my kit, I slumped, once more, off the summit, fatigued and drenched with sweat.

Brown came up to me from behind, catching me by surprise. 'Para's really struggling.'

'Is he?' I was straining to stand upright.

'He's run out of water.'

Before I could say anything, Brown had walked on, past me, keeping his hard-earned elevation. I looked again at my map and felt sure the best way was straight down: I could see the barn in the distance. What was Brown doing?

I dropped quickly, but Brown strode on boldly in a large horseshoe, along a ridge running away from the summit. Several other men followed him. I jerked down a dry, rocky waterfall. Fowkes came up towards me.

'Third time?' I groaned.

'Yes,' he said. His Scots burr seemed to become more pro- nounced when he was tired. 'Just keep moving. Just keep moving. Don't stop.'

At the bottom of the waterfall I stumbled across a soldier. He was lying face down in the short grass, at the foot of a pile of huge dislodged boulders. The coloured rocks, worn smooth by the passage of water, lay jumbled and bleached in the sun, like the pebbles in a dried-up river bed.

'Are you all right?' I said, running down to him and dropping my weapon.

He groaned and rolled over onto his back, defenceless like a fallen ram. I recognized him immediately. He was a tall, powerful man with short fair hair, which was always neatly combed. He was in Two Squadron.

'I'm all right,' he said, falling onto his side and slipping a bit further down the grassy bank. His bergen was still on his back and it dragged him down like a tumbling stone. He came to a halt against a pile of scree. 'I went too fast at the beginning. I'm stopping at the next RV. I'm through. You go on. I'll be all right.'

'Are you sure?' Both of us were being extraordinarily polite.

'Yes. You keep going. I've had enough. Tell them I'm coming.' He began to roll forwards down the hill again.

I put on my cap-comforter, scrabbled down the last few hundred feet of the mountain and ran along the dry cart-track to the barn. After I had given out all my details, and collected the grid reference for the next RV, which was the summit again, I pointed out the dazed recruit to the corporals. We watched as he tumbled, got up, fell again, twisted, turned, stood up and finally tripped his way down the hillside.

'Waster,' the corporal said, as he watched this spectacle. And then, turning to me, 'Go on. You carry on. I'll go and get Rambo out there.'

As I began to climb again, Brown came around the hillside towards me.

'Where did you go?' I asked. 'You had me worried.'

'I went around the ridge,' he replied, looking dejected. His pale, bulging cheeks gave his face a bloated look, like a body washed up by the tide. 'I can't think why I did it.' His thick lips quivered.

'The RV's just down the track. You can't miss it.'

We separated and I continued to climb the mountain for the third time. But I could not see straight: sweat was in my eyes and I suddenly felt light-headed. I passed a recruit about a kilometre from the summit.

'I can't make it,' he said, turning round. 'I'm going back to the barn.'

The sun poured down and the scree radiated the heat. I carried on and the recruit got smaller and smaller, as he walked the seven kilometres back to the penultimate RV.

Another recruit sat on his bergen, a few hundred feet down from Scott. He had taken off his cap-comforter and was looking, across the hills, at the sea in the distance. His smock was unzipped to the waist, and his chest bare and glistening with sweat. He held a water-bottle, idly, in his hand. Every so often, he took a sip.

'It's beautiful, isn't it?' he said, as I stepped up to him. 'Look at the colours.'

I turned to look and saw hills, fields and farms, in shades of green and brown. A few wisps of delicate white cloud lay draped across the sky.

'Don't let the OC see you,' I said. 'He'll go spare if he catches you sitting down.'

'I don't care. I'm not going any further. Look at the colours.'

'You can't sit here all day,' I said, bending forwards in an attempt to relieve my shoulders for a second or two.

'Yes I can. Look, it's beautiful.'

I pressed on upwards, my load pulling me down.

'Good effort, Ballinger,' said Scott, when I came up to him for what I prayed was the last time. 'Straight back down to the OC and that's it. Cordwell's catching you so don't lose it now.'

Cordwell overtook me half-way down and I came in fourth. Fowkes came first and Cordwell second. Someone in another squadron took third place. Brown came fifth. Para and White came in later and Avery was near the back. Scott gave Avery what Brown referred to as 'an official warning'. But Avery had completed the circuit within the time.

We sat, at the end of the march, in some pine woods. They were bordered in the south by a lay-by and in the north by a mountain stream. The stream was wide, and deep enough to allow a man to lie down comfortably and enjoy the soothing coolness. In the woods, which were on a slight slope, a variety of bashas had been constructed. Mostly they were designed to create shade rather than prevent rain. Some were empty and some were occupied.

It was later in the day and cooler than it had been. All the men were tired. There was very little movement. Few ventured beyond their bashas. Significant disturbance occurred only when there was a new arrival. Some men were asleep. Some were nursing their feet or the bergen burns on their backs. All semblance of urgency and aggression had gone. Some were cleaning their weapons, carefully removing the working parts and polishing them. Occasionally, the click of a reassembly could be heard through the woods. Other men were sitting by their hexi-stoves cooking in a state of contentment. Some were lying down on their sides to cook. A few were daydreaming.

I sat in my basha talking to Para, who had stripped to the waist to expose his sores to the air.

'That was the hardest thing I have ever done,' he said.

'What about the Para course?'

'That's different. There's nothing like this in it.'

'Imagine what Long Drag must be like.'

'Yes. Fucking awful,' he said, pulling at his blisters. 'It's about twice as long as that. I kept thinking about it all the way round.' He looked down at his feet again and, taking a needle from his sewing kit, began to burst his blisters until they bled.

An hour later the last recruit came in and fell, like a winded man, at White's feet. White made him a cup of tea. Falstaff, who was the only man standing, noticed White's gesture and, smiling beneath his dense moustache, said, 'Thank you.'

He strode around between the bashas, his thick black hair shining in the dappled sunlight. He looked almost operatic in his boots, camouflage trousers and green T-shirt. An S-shaped meerschaum was clamped between his teeth and he puffed out smoke with an air of amusement. He ambled about from basha to basha talking and joking, as if we were his ragamuffins. His style was short sentences, witty remarks, and smiles. He was not a man for bellyaching laughter.

'What's this?' he asks, 'a Lawrence of Arabia basha? Where are the camels?' But, when he peered in, the shelter was empty.

He stepped idly over to me. 'What's your previous military experience?'

'None, sir,' I said, pleased that he did not, apparently, remember our previous encounter. 'I was a civilian.'

His eyes twinkled: I was his for the taking; perfectly plastic, uncorrupted by other regiments. He was delighted by the surprise. 'Well, you have obviously got one and a half brains,' he said, but then, realizing he had been too generous, added, 'well, either that or half a brain,' and laughed.

My turn over, he stepped across the narrow furrow of pine needles, to speak to Para.

'How are you getting on?'

Falstaff knew Para through his father, who was also in the regular SAS. All three of them had fought in the Falklands War. Para smiled and looked at his feet.

'This regiment does not vote with its feet,' said Falstaff, grinning. 'When I did 22 Selection I used to sleep in between marches. I should get your head down until someone tells you to move.'

'Listen, lads,' the OC said, calling a sudden and informal parade in the lay-by. 'One bloke's gone missing. Has anyone seen Wilson?'

'I saw him just below the top, sir,' said one recruit.

'What time?'

'About five o'clock, sir.'

'Where did he go?'

'He was walking down the mountain, sir. Said he was going to the farm. I thought it was the next RV after the summit.'

'Fucking hell. Do you know which farm?'

'Think so, sir.'

'Come here and show me. Bring your map! OK, the rest of you, get back to your bashas.'

The recruit gave the OC the grid reference of the farm he thought Wilson had walked to, and Falstaff, taking the map, set off in the OC's Land Rover.

Two hours later, as the sun was setting behind the ridge of the mountains, we stood wearily and once again on parade. Our numbers were reduced by half. More than half of the men had completed the day march, but a large number of these could not bring themselves to go on again, marching between another set of RVs during the night. They voluntarily withdrew from the course.

'Listen, lads,' the OC said. 'This course is decimated. Half the blokes have dropped out today. This weekend always thins out the wasters, but, fucking hell, this is ridiculous. I still can't believe this,

lads, but Wilson went to a farmhouse for tea. Fucking tea! Just went
up to the door and asked the farmer's wife. The PSI found him with
his feet up in front of the fire – in front of the fucking fire! – talking,
as if he had all the time in the world! What the fuck does he think
this is? The Girl Guides?'

The OC was so excited he could not stand still. Only when he
had finished talking about Wilson did he calm down.

'Now, lads,' he said, 'Selection really begins.'

We stood to attention, with our bergens just behind us. The OC
walked up and down the depleted rows of recruits. He stopped at
Para. There was something very slightly different about Para's
boots.

'Are these your issued boots?' he growled, staring at Para.

'No, sir,' said Para.

'Why not?'

'They're broken, sir.'

'So fucking what? Every man on this course wears issued boots.
Is that clear? No personal kit. If I catch you wearing those again
you're off the course. No man on this course has an unfair
advantage. Is that clear?'

'Sir.'

The OC paired us up for the night march and put White and me
together.

'Today thinned me out, all right,' said White, recalling the OC's
words, as we stumbled painfully through the black, starry night,
searching for yet another RV.

Scott woke us up at six-thirty. Neither White nor I could easily
stand. We fell in with the other recruits for PT. The exercises seized
our bodies with a vengeance but we were too fatigued to know
what we were doing. I survived to stand, in agony, on parade. Scott
inspected my mess tins. The bottom of one of them did not shine
like a jewel in the sunlight. For this, he forced me to do fifty press-
ups, each time pushing my nose into the dirty canteen.

Eight of us, weak, sore, stiff and blistered, drove back to the
barracks on Sunday afternoon. The rest of the squadron had failed

and had been sent home on Saturday. Scott was incensed that men in his squadron, men that he had trained, had failed, and that some had withdrawn because of blisters.

'*Blisters!* A bloke escaped from hospital with no legs and we have lost recruits through bloody blisters! *Wasters*. Fucking wasters.'

Ordering us into a row he made us jump, on the parade-ground, in time, first on one foot and then on the other. We had to slap each thigh aggressively, as it became horizontal, and shout, '*My fucking feet don't hurt. My fucking feet don't hurt.*'

OUT OF STEAM

The loser at the hazard, when the game breaks up,
Sadder and sorrier lingers on alone,
Re-plays each throw, and drinks of wisdom's cup.

Dante

The eighth man in our squadron to survive the weekend stood over six feet tall and weighed nearly fourteen stone. With big bones and densely developed muscles he was extremely strong. And yet, in his civilian clothes and smart suit, he looked like the humble civil servant he was. On drill nights he arrived carrying, in one hand, a small leather briefcase that folded over the top like a school satchel. In the other he carried a sports bag, with a capacity larger than our bergens, filled with kit. He had short ginger hair and an angelic smile. Only when he had just had his hair cut did his head look slightly small on his formidable frame. His surname was Sampson. No one used his Christian name. For the duration of the night marches he had often been paired with the small, gristly Para. White and I always laughed if we met them on the hills, for Sampson usually led the way, swinging his bergen, like a small knapsack, from his strong shoulders. Para trailed him, dwarfed by his bergen, taking two steps to every one of Sampson's.

Of the eight of us only Sampson and I had no previous military experience. Sampson had tried to join the Royal Marines when he left school, but at the last minute decided to go to a Polytechnic and read Accounting. His girlfriend was an aerobics instructor.

As I stood on the barrack-square talking to Sampson, Fowkes tipped his fetid kit out onto his poncho for inspection.

'Don't you wash your stuff from one weekend to the next?' Sampson asked.

Fowkes' boots rolled to the side of his poncho. The wet leather had gone white with mould, and his smock and camouflage trousers smelt of stale sweat.

'I haven't got time for that,' said Fowkes intently. 'I've got a business to run.' He bent down in his torn, bespoke, pin-striped suit and arranged the jumble of clammy clothes into some sort of pile for inspection.

'Thank God we've got you in the squadron,' said Cordwell. 'I don't feel so bad now.'

'What's wrong?' said Fowkes, pleased with his hasty arrangement. 'It'll only get dirty again this weekend.'

Two more drill nights had passed without incident and the eight of us stood in front of the squadron four-tonner, for the start of another weekend. It was a warm Friday evening, and most of us had left work early to be at the barracks on time. We waited, in our civilian clothes, for Scott to arrive.

Two or three lime trees grew on the edge of the square, and as we stood talking the leaves fluttered in the breeze. Eight ponchos had been laid out, with eight sets of kit arranged on top. Every man organized his belongings in a different way: there was no pattern.

'I wonder who's screwing my girlfriend this weekend?' said Cordwell.

'One thing's for sure,' said Avery, 'it's not you.'

'I could be surfing in Bude, tonight,' said Cordwell, staring dejectedly at his small pile of belongings. 'All my mates are going. They kept saying, "Come on, it's only the TA. Surely you can make it."'

'What did you say?'

'I had to apologize. They thought I was insane.'

When the conversation had died down, and the men had separated again to double-check their kit, White sidled up to me and said, 'Can I have a word?' His blue eyes squinted in the sun, and his blond, curly hair had been left uncombed. When we were out of earshot of the others, he said, 'My girlfriend's threatening to leave me.'

'Why?' I asked.

'She says this takes up too much time. And when we do see each other I'm always tired.'

'But surely you're not going to let her leave you?'

'I don't know what to do. We've been together for years.'

'It's not worth losing her,' I said.

'I know. We're supposed to be sailing in the Cyclades after Long Drag, in the week before Camp.'

We turned and began to walk back across the square towards our ponchos.

'I had hoped to combine this with my elective,' he said, sounding optimistic again. 'I'm going to Botswana and I want to be a doctor for this regiment.'

When White and I joined the others, Fowkes said, 'I'm trying to get a group together for self-defence classes. Are you interested?'

White laughed.

'Come on, it's only martial arts. A ten-week course. You'd be a certified bodyguard at the end.'

Sampson looked dubious. 'I've done judo and karate.'

'What about you?' Fowkes asked, turning to me.

'No time,' I said. 'It's bad enough trying to do this.'

'I'm keen,' said Avery, straightening his tie.

'Cordwell?'

'No. I boxed at Cambridge. I've had enough bloody noses to last me a fucking lifetime.'

'Brown?'

'Hey, Brown!' Cordwell shouted. 'Don't look so miserable.'

Brown was bending over his kit, away from the seven of us, checking his pocket torch. He turned and nodded, but failed to smile.

'Forget it,' said Cordwell to Fowkes. 'He's not interested.'

When Brown had finished he came over to us, and said, 'Soon be off. The sooner we get going the better.'

'You know,' said Cordwell, looking up at him. 'I don't know why you do this. You're always so fucking miserable. Cheer up, for God's sake.'

Brown smiled.

When Scott arrived we loaded the four-tonner and drove to a different location.

'Listen in,' said Scott, standing on a kerbstone at first light the following morning. 'What we want is lunatics. What you cunts need is a bloody good fight on Saturday night. Aggression. Speed and aggression; that's what it's all about. I want to see you fucking move this weekend.'

'One thing, lads,' said the OC, coming through the woods and interrupting him, 'don't get arrested. I want you here for the next exercise. Corporal Scott's right, though. It's no good walking. Some of you are just bimbling around the hills. On this exercise I want to see you run, run, run.'

The aim of the exercise was to provide practice in navigation and build up stamina by carrying a fifty-pound bergen, in addition to the usual Belgian weapon and webbing, over arduous terrain. During the day we were to walk alone.

It was a short walk – thirty kilometres across country – but because there was no aim other than to build up stamina, it was uneventful. I moved at well above the minimum pace and finished the circuit with two hours to spare, but relatively I performed badly. I was one and a half hours behind Fowkes, who was the first man. At the second RV Scott told me I had some work to do: I had lost the front runners. At the next RV the OC called me over. 'You all right? Injured?'

'No, sir,' I said.

'Then put the bloody lead down.' He looked down at me from the top of his Land Rover and laid aside his telescope. 'I want to see scorch marks. *Run.*'

Tired and fed up, I finished the day march in about seven hours.

After a short rest, the OC put us into pairs for the night march. He put Avery and me together. For several hours we battled in

thick mist through knee-deep grass. Avery's boots had rubbed the
skin off his heels and his socks were soaked in blood, but he
continued to joke about our slow progress. On tracks he could not
run. When Scott appeared, in the dead of night, and in the middle
of nowhere, he was livid. He screamed at Avery for not going fast
enough and at me, for not punching Avery in the face and telling
him to get a move on.

We woke after one and a half hours' sleep at six-thirty. Sampson
said he dreamt he was walking through moon grass and when he
woke he was. For the first time since the course began, the
squadron returned to the barracks with the same number of
recruits: no one had failed.

All eight of us climbed into the back of the four-tonner and we
rattled back down the motorway towards the barracks. We sat, four
against each side, in our civilian sports clothes. Few wore any
footwear. Eight pairs of feet had suffered and no one stood on them
more than they had to.

Para and Sampson had tied the canvas flap down to the tail-gate,
in an attempt to prevent the exhaust fumes from being sucked back
inside. We sat, accordingly, in semi-darkness.

'This is the best bit of the weekend,' said Brown, stretching out.
'This is the bit I look forward to.' As he spoke, he lay down on his
military sleeping bag. He had spread it out, across the truck, to
cushion the ribbed floor. Resting his head on his kit bag, he opened
the *Sunday Times* he had bought when we had stopped at a service
station.

Para and Sampson had split a *Sunday Sport* and the pages were
scattered across the floor.

'I can't make the PSI out,' I said, turning to Avery. 'He is exactly
how I imagined Falstaff to look.'

'You mean his size?' said Avery, lowering Brown's colour
supplement.

'He's fat. It's not exactly how you'd expect a soldier in 22 to
look.'

'He's 22's best sniper,' said Avery. 'Don't be deceived by his
appearance.'

'He got injured in Northern Ireland,' said Para, joining in. 'He was in hospital for nearly a year. Couldn't exercise for a long time afterwards. That's why they put him in charge of Selection. He's got years of experience. He's a fucking good shot.'

Cordwell picked up a few sheets of Para's paper and scanned the pictures. He said, 'I wonder if my girlfriend will be in tonight?'

'My missis won't be, that's for sure,' said Para. He sat next to the tail-gate and was tightening one of the canvas buckles that held the back down.

'Why not?' Cordwell asked.

'I threw a clock at her just before I left on Friday, and walked out. Stupid bitch. She hates the army. We got divorced after the Falklands, but then we got back together again. Fucking mistake that was.'

Para rummaged around in his kit bag and pulled out a packet of cigarettes. He offered one to Cordwell. As he bent forward, his T-shirt rose up the small of his back to reveal a bloody scar the size of a man's palm: his bergen, wet with salty sweat, had acted like an abrasive and, sliding around on his back, had slowly rubbed the skin away.

'Two more weekends to Long Drag,' said Fowkes.

'Yes,' I said. 'Sometimes I wonder if it's possible.'

'If Scott can do it, so can you,' said Brown, looking around the side of his newspaper.

'Have you ever walked forty or fifty miles in one day?' I asked. 'Let alone with a fifty-pound bergen, and the rest.'

'I did thirty-six once,' said Brown. 'It took all day. But I didn't have a rucksack.'

'I tried forty, last year, on the Pennines,' I said. 'It was terrible.'

'How far do you think it is?' Fowkes asked.

'A fucking long way,' said Para. 'Even you will feel it.'

'I don't know I'll make it,' said Avery. 'You've got to average three K an hour. That's faster than I've been managing so far.'

'You'll be all right,' said Brown.

'Yes, but Avery's got Scott to contend with,' I said.

'Yes. That bastard hates me.'

'If Scott fails me,' said Para, 'I'm going to fucking smash him.'

Para and Cordwell finished their cigarettes, and the smoke gradually cleared as the wind blew through the holes in the canvas.

'What does your employer think of the TA?' I asked Brown.

'Oh, they don't mind. One woman raises her eyebrows when I leave early during the week for drill nights. On Fridays she always says, "Off with the SAS are we?" and bursts out laughing.'

'That sounds a bit close to the knuckle,' I said. 'You want to watch it.'

'She's all right. She's got no idea. She thinks I'm in the Catering Corps or something. I'd love to tell her. That would shut her up.'

'Can you get the time off for Camp, if we get that far?'

'Yes. I get an extra week for military service. I'll take the other week out of my annual leave.'

'Same for me,' said Avery. 'I had to see my manager on Friday afternoon. He kept saying, "We expect an above average commitment in this bank, Avery".'

'What did you say?'

'Nothing. I was too bloody anxious to get here on time. I kept looking at my watch.'

'I'll have to get a certificate from the OC,' said Para. 'Otherwise, they won't believe me. I've only just started work. I've been unemployed for two fucking years.'

'You want to join the civil service,' said Sampson, looking up for the first time. 'They're excellent for leave. I get three or four weeks extra for military courses. And I work flexi-time.'

'That's the bloody civil service for you,' said Avery, smiling. 'It's no wonder the country's in such a state.'

Suddenly the driver braked and we all lurched forwards towards the cab. Para pulled back the canvas flap and started to clamber out. 'We're here.'

'Wake up, White,' said Cordwell, shaking his shoulder. 'We're at the barracks.'

We unloaded the kit and washed the four-tonner. Fowkes, Sampson and Para disappeared together. 'You're quiet,' I said to White as he, too, turned to go.

'Oh . . . It's nothing . . .' He hesitated as if to continue, but then Brown came in and he left. Avery and Cordwell went off to try to find the Storeman and I was left in the changing room with Brown.

'Well then, are you a lunatic?' I asked, remembering Scott.

'Of course not,' he said, clutching his civilian shoes. 'Are you? All this aggression stuff is rubbish. It's like the OC said, you've got to be able to turn yourself on and off, like a light switch. What this regiment is about,' continued Brown, as he unlaced his training shoes, 'is self-control and discipline. They want balanced, well-informed human beings, men who can make decisions. It's all about sizing up a situation, rapidly, and then acting.'

Avery and Cordwell came back down the corridor and dropped their kit bags onto the benches.

'I'm having a shower,' said Cordwell. He undressed quickly and dropped his clothes on the floor. He stood, naked, in front of us and said, 'You know, I had to walk with Fowkes last night. I've never known anyone push himself so fucking hard. I had to run to keep up. He's the only man I've ever met who is totally oblivious to pain.'

Cordwell walked into the shower, and Brown and I finished changing.

'Right, I'm off,' said Avery. 'I'm going home to watch *Platoon*. I got the video last week.'

'See you,' said Brown.

We met again, later in the week, on our drill night.

Scott continued to take our lessons. The lecture this week was on 'The Theory of Small Arms Fire'. He introduced us to a range of concepts such as culminating points, catches, grazes and beaten zones. When firing from a hundred metres, he said, aim four inches above the heart.

I asked Avery about this while we changed for PT. Instinctively, I would have aimed for the heart. Avery seemed pleased when I posed my question.

'I had to think about that, too,' he said. 'It's because the round describes a parabolic trajectory through space. At a hundred metres, the bullet is four inches below the line of departure. The culminating point is the maxima on the curve.'

'That was a bloody good lesson,' said Cordwell, walking in through the door. 'I always wondered what the purpose of flanking was. I thought it was just to piss-off the gun group.'

'It's to maximize the overlap between the beaten zone and the target area,' said Avery.

'Fucking hell!' said Sampson, dropping his running shoes.

THE SUN HAS GOT HIS HAT ON

*I live in a society of men who take habitual care
of their bodies, and temper them by games and
exercise and diet to a dry degree of splendour.*

T. E. Lawrence

Ten days later, after another drill night, the eight of us left the barracks for the sixth test weekend. It was almost a year to the day since I had completed the first five-mile run, and I was not yet a third of the way through the course. There were eight of us left and this, the OC said, was an unusually high number. The original numbers were vague but we estimated them to be between thirty and forty for One Squadron. The numbers in the other squadrons had fallen far more quickly, and were still falling. Our numbers had, for the first time, stabilized. Scott and the OC appeared pleased, but the end of the course was a very long way off and anything, they kept telling us, could still happen.

The following morning, I stood on familiar terrain in North Wales listening to the OC's orders. Six or seven men were all that remained in Two Squadron, and four or five in Three Squadron. One man remained in Four, and in Five there were no recruits left on the course. The man in Four Squadron always stood on his own, at the end of the row, with his bergen on one side and his corporal on the other. The concept of a one-man squadron frequently made the OC laugh, but the recruit received the same treatment as the rest of us. Inspection of Four Squadron, however, was always much quicker than inspection of One Squadron.

'Listen, lads,' the OC said, at the end of his brief. 'You may see a small man, up there, on the hills today. He is the Colonel of 22 SAS. If you do see him, keep running. Don't stop for a chat, unless he speaks to you. If he does, treat him with the respect he deserves: he is an extremely experienced soldier. But don't be frightened, lads. Speak up if he talks to you: he's a soldier's man.'

After parade and kit check we were divided into three groups. Each group would follow one of three routes; red, green or blue. I was green. My name and number were called at eight-thirty. Falstaff transcribed my details onto his large white control chart and I was off.

Three words bounced around my head: run, run, run; and I ran all day, except where it was too steep to do so. I made mistakes. I went down and up when I should have stayed on the same contour. Sometimes I went unnecessarily high before dropping; but I also made some good decisions and, for much of the day, I averaged about six kilometres an hour.

At the end of the afternoon I ran across a disused quarry, my steps echoing in the deep chamber, and up onto a gravel track on the far side. I could see the RV in the distance, a thousand metres away. I guessed it was the last RV, because of the preponderance of four-tonners parked on the grass, and, therefore, that it was manned by Falstaff and the OC. As I left the protection of the quarry, I suddenly realized that I was in full view of the OC.

I ran. My bergen bounced up and down on my shoulders and my knees jolted like the chassis of a bus with no shock absorbers, as I threw each foot forward onto the gravel.

When I came in, Scott lifted my bergen off my shoulders and hung it from his balance, which was fixed to the side of the Storeman's four-tonner. It swung out, like a crane above a Victorian grain store. Scott called out the weights.

'Bergen: fifty-six pounds. Webbing: ten pounds. Weapon: ten pounds.' Falstaff took the smouldering meerschaum from his lips, smiled and wrote down the figures against my name on his large white chart. 'Not bad for seventy-six pounds,' grunted Scott, as he passed me back my kit.

'Is there any water?' I asked.

'In the jerry cans, at the back of the squadron four-tonner.'

I walked over to the truck and, with my bergen still on my shoulders, I pulled a water-bottle from my webbing. Before I got to the water supply, however, a small man with short grey hair darted round the back of the truck and took the container from me. He filled it from the jerry can.

'Well done,' the Colonel said, as he passed it back to me. But before I could respond he disappeared again, back around the side of the four-tonner, and into the OC's tent.

Three hours later, the night march began, and the routine of racing between RVs continued.

I became half conscious when the birds started singing. I turned my face and opened my eyes, and then, exhausted, closed them again. I felt chilled but, through my eyelids, I could see that the sun was shining brightly. I tried once more. A cold breeze stung my face and made my eyes water. The wind caught the fallen leaves and they fluttered across my green sleeping bag.

Avery looked at me: he too was still in his sleeping bag. 'You know, Chamberlain declared war on Germany fifty years ago this morning.'

'Yes.' But I had forgotten when I had woken up and seen the sky. It had hardly seemed possible. I stepped out of my sleeping bag and onto the cold, wet dew.

PT began abruptly. We ran to a car-park about one mile from our basha camp, where we were split into teams for a selection of relay races. These were preferable to individual exercises, for not only were they more fun, but they made the forty-five minutes allotted to PT pass more quickly. After the relay races Scott paced us to the top of a four-hundred-foot hill and back.

Finally, we fell in, in three ranks, on the edge of the car-park, ready to run back to the bashas. We all wore plimsolls, camouflaged trousers and T-shirts, and we held identical Belgian weapons across our chests in the high-port position. A quiet track led off from the gravel car-park and wound its way slowly up the hillside.

It was a tranquil Sunday morning. The sun was warming the countryside and a thick ground mist swirled around the valley, like seaweed sliding back and forth in a roving sea. The dark, quarried slate was damp with dew. There was no traffic and there were no civilians.

'Good effort, lads,' said the small Welshman, who was the corporal accompanying Four Squadron. He stood in the middle of the track. 'But the OC thinks you lot are fucking miserable. We'll show him who's fucking miserable. I'm going to lead the way back to the basha site. I want you to sing, with me, "The Sun Has Got His Hat On". We'll show him, lads.'

We ran along the track and steadily climbed the hillside. When we were nearing the final bend before the campsite, the corporal ran a few yards ahead and then turned around. Running backwards and facing us, he said, 'Come on, fill your lungs with air:

> The sun has got his hat on,
> Hip hip hip hooray,
> The sun has got his hat on,
> And is coming out to play.

> Then we'll all be happy,
> Hip hip hip hooray,
> 'Cause the sun has got his hat on,
> And is coming out to play.

The OC smiled and looked across at the Colonel who, very quickly, winked at Falstaff.

'Well done, lads,' said the OC with one eye on the Colonel. 'You have now entered what I call the "Reasonably Hard" category. One Squadron has done well this weekend.' He nodded at the eight of us. 'We've not lost anyone this time, and we've got some good times. Run, lads, run, that's what it's all about.

'In two weeks' time it's the test weekend. We'll be watching you even more closely. The week after that, in three weeks' time, lads, it's Long Drag – that fucking great leveller of men. In 22 it used to be called Endurance. You will not stop. If you stop once, you stop twice.

'Those of you who can do sums have probably realized that the format is a little bit different. There will be no weekend off, in between the test weekend and Long Drag. You go straight into it, lads.

'There are two more drill nights before the test weekend when you'll revise your drills for the weapons test. The weapons test takes place in the week before Long Drag. It's a lot to take in, so listen very carefully to what your corporals tell you. They've been there before, although it might not seem like it at times. They know what it's like. Use them. If you don't understand anything, for fuck's sake ask. Don't come to me if you fail and say, "I forgot to ask, sir". It's up to you.'

He took his beige beret out of his pocket with a flourish and pointed the badge at us. 'It's fucking hard to get this,' he said, squeezing the beret. 'Fucking hard.' For a second or two there was silence and then, in a quivering voice and with his hand very slightly shaking, he said, 'You've got to fucking want it, lads. You've got to fucking want it.'

After the debrief, we sat down in our civilian clothes on the verge bordering the slate track, and waited for the squadron four-tonner to arrive. Cordwell lay back on the warm grass and quickly fell asleep.

Brown said, 'In three weeks' time, it'll all be over.'

'Selection, yes,' said Para. 'You've still got Camp and Continuation to get through. And that's another six months, at least.'

'I've got to get through, now,' said White.

'Haven't we all.' Para took a cigarette out of his top pocket and held it in his hand. Turning on his side, he noticed Fowkes fumbling with his few remaining rations. 'What the fuck are you doing?'

'Eating my rations.' Fowkes was munching his way through a cold bacon burger.

'I don't know how you can bear to eat that stuff,' said Sampson.

Fowkes sat, with his legs stretched out in front of him, leaning over his box of rations. 'What's wrong? Can't waste good food.'

Sampson looked disgusted. 'Didn't you eat earlier?'

'No. I wasn't going to use my mess tins. It's the only way I can keep them clean enough for inspection.'

Para and Sampson laughed.

'Not many people fail Long Drag,' said Para, lighting his cigarette. 'It's getting that far, that's the hard bit.' He drew his knees up to his chest and put his arms around his shins. The smouldering cigarette dangled between his fingers. He took another puff and peered across the valley. 'Still, it's a fucking long way.'

'It wouldn't be so bad,' I said, 'if you knew how far it was.'

'That's why you don't fucking know,' said Para.

'By the way, Avery,' said Fowkes, 'I've booked the self-defence classes. They start on the first Thursday after Camp – eight o'clock.'

'Thanks,' said Avery. 'Remind me nearer the time.' Avery lay, propped up on one shoulder, cleaning his fingernails with his penknife. 'Why did you leave the Paras, Fowkes?' he asked.

Two or three people rolled over to look at Fowkes.

'I liked being out on the hills. The best bit was walking in the Cairngorms.' As he said this, he relapsed into a stronger Scottish accent. 'But then it changed. We started doing more and more shooting. I kept saying to myself, "Why am I doing this?" I was also doing a Hotel and Catering course at the time and I got a job in a restaurant in Hong Kong, so I went.'

'But you're here,' I said, lying on my stomach and facing him.

'Yes. It's good for you. Gets you out in the weekends. Teaches you to appreciate the good things. You've got to push yourself. It's good discipline.'

'Back to my fucking missis tonight,' said Para, changing the subject. 'Mind you, have you seen Sampson's bit?'

'She's gone off the TA,' said Sampson. 'I told her that if I get through to Camp, we'd have to cancel our holiday. I told her this comes first. If she doesn't like it, tough shit.'

Avery laughed. 'She's an aerobics instructor, isn't she?'

'Yes.'

'Is she very fit?'

'No. She's not fit enough. Last week, just as we were getting going, she said, "I've got to stop, I'm tired now." '

'Come on, lads,' said Scott, 'here comes the four-tonner.'

TESTS

What doth gravity out of his bed at midnight?
Shall I give him his answer?

                          Shakespeare

At midnight it was warm and dark in the woods, and raining hard. First light was due at ten-past five. Brown and I sat on our bergens, together and alone, under a tall pine tree. Fourteen mountains rose three thousand feet upwards into the darkness. This was a night march in pairs, across North Wales and against the clock. It was the test weekend, the penultimate exercise before Long Drag. We sat in silence waiting for the order to move. The slowest men had already started. Fowkes and Cordwell were the fastest pair and they sat quietly elsewhere in the woods. At last our turn came and we lifted our bergens and weapons out into the rain. Falstaff, sitting comfortably in the back of his Land Rover, with his pipe in one hand and a pen in another, logged us out. We were off.

The first hill was deceptively steep and exposed. A wicked wind howled across the top, and the rain swept across the ridge horizontally. We found the first RV, a lone four-tonner camouflaged in a depression, quickly and without error. A corporal gave us another grid reference and we set off again into the night.

Half walking, half running, we made our way to the bottom of a valley. We could hear water gurgling in small rock pools and through deep channels in the hillside, but we could not see it. The mist and rain blew into our faces and our eyes watered in the wind.

But then, momentarily, the clouds broke, and a full moon shone through. A shaft of intense light fell like a spotlight on the dark scene below. Suddenly, the trickling water sparkled white and the small, black puddles in the muddy sheep tracks glimmered like glass. Great arcs of light fell across the grey crags, and the clefts slunk further back into shadow.

We were alone in a monochrome scene. Laden with kit we pressed on through a landscape awash with water and mud. We splashed our way down the hillside and across the slush at the bottom. Brown was reminded of an old black-and-white First World War film he had seen. I thought about the photographs of the trenches I had seen, and of Wilfred Owen and his death crossing the Sambre Canal. As soon as the clouds parted they drew together again, like curtains shutting out light. We were left in darkness. More rain fell.

In the hour before dawn we struggled to find a track and when we did find it, we ran to make up for lost time. No sooner had we started when I tripped and fell. Fortunately I was not injured. Two minutes later Brown did the same, but he smashed his face on a rock, cutting his nose, eyelid and forehead. He lost consciousness for a second or two, but was soon on his feet again, swaying under the weight of his bergen. I gave him my handkerchief; his face was streaked with blood and muddy water. We were separated at the third RV, for by then it was daylight. I made it to the final RV by six-fifteen and Brown came in minutes later. We had covered nineteen kilometres, in total darkness and steady rain, in just over five and a half hours. We passed.

Each recruit was given a two-hour rest between completing the night march and beginning the day march, but as Brown pointed out those were the fastest two hours he had known.

At eight-fifteen I was off again. Thirty or forty kilometres to go, I told myself, and you've done it. There were only four RVs in total. One recruit who had walked the route on a previous selection course had – illegally – shown me his map. It did not look too bad, but to my surprise and disappointment it took a long time. On the Pennines I could cover fifty kilometres in about nine hours, but not now. Such was the effect of a pair of sloppy army boots, a crippling bergen, webbing and a weapon. None of the stretches was easy. I hesitated more than I should have done. The last leg, which I thought would be trivial, was seemingly endless moon grass. When the end came it was not a second too soon.

I woke to the pleasing pit-pat of rain on the roof of my basha. Raindrops fell off the sloping sides and onto the wet grass. Still lying in my sleeping bag I pulled a mess tin out of the side of my bergen, and set it carefully on the bumpy ground to catch the rainwater. I made a ripple in the canvas so that I could direct the flow. Soon my mess tin was full and I had enough water to shave for parade.

Inspection was without incident, save for the fact that we were very few in number. The eight of us had survived, but Two Squadron had lost two recruits and Three Squadron had lost one. The men who had failed had feared exposure and had stopped at the nearest RV.

Of the original one hundred and fifty, eighteen recruits remained. We sat in the drizzle on our bergens, in a semicircle, around the back of Falstaff's Land Rover. He had parked it on the leeward side of some trees on the edge of the woods, and his control schedule swung from the back. Pinned over the top of it was a large waterproofed map of Yorkshire. Every man sat forward and struggled to read the place names that had been circled, but Falstaff deliberately kept the map too far away.

'Well done, lads,' said the OC, standing in front of the map and addressing all eighteen of us. 'You've won a place on Long Drag.'

Fowkes, who was sitting by me, turned and whispered in my ear, 'He makes it sound like a holiday for two in Paris.'

When the OC had finished his brief, Falstaff very quickly unhooked his map and pushed it out of sight into the back of his Land Rover.

The eight of us in One Squadron met again during the week, on a drill night that was earlier than usual, for our weapons test.

'I want the best blokes, first,' said Scott coming into our classroom. 'Para, Ballinger, follow me.'

We followed him across the barrack-square, through the green doors, outside of which, nearly a year ago, I had waited so expectantly, and up the stone stairs to the drill hall where we had had our medicals on April Fool's Day. At the top of the stairs Para turned to me and said, 'He doesn't really think we're the best.'

'Of course he doesn't,' I said. 'He said it to upset the others, not to compliment us.'

Scott came back across the drill hall scowling beneath his beret. 'OK, Para, you over there, and you, Ballinger, over in that corner.' He pointed to two corners hidden from each other by screens that would have served, admirably, to conceal an Edwardian bath.

I walked over to the examination corner, just to the left of the list of regimental VCs, and was greeted by Falstaff. A loaded weapon lay on the floor.

'Off you go,' said Falstaff. 'You can assume it's not booby-trapped.'

When I had made the weapon safe, I had to strip it against the clock, name all the parts, and reassemble it with a blindfold. I demonstrated the firing positions we had been taught, and talked about the principles of marksmanship, the different methods of engaging targets and the adjustments one has to make for wind speeds and directions.

When I had finished, and when I had repeatedly loaded and unloaded a magazine of rounds, again against the clock, Falstaff said, 'You've not done this before, have you?'

'No, sir.'

'It shows. You're not as confident as you need to be. But don't worry, that'll come. It's Camp in ten days' time. You'll do more shooting then than a regular infantry soldier will do in three years.'

Brown and Avery went next, but Brown came back a few minutes later. Falstaff had failed him, not on a safety error, for which he would have been dismissed immediately from the course, but because he had failed to fill a magazine fast enough. When everyone else had been tested, Brown was given one more chance. Scott made him load and unload a magazine, repeatedly, on the dusty classroom floor for more than thirty minutes until his turn came.

He passed.

At half-past nine Scott took us for what we assumed would be a last and gentle session of PT. Long Drag was only two days away and we were still weak from the test weekend. No such thoughts, however, went through Scott's mind. He paced us, for sixteen miles, around the back streets of London. It was well past eleven o'clock when we finally returned to the barracks.

We sat on the wooden benches in the changing room, dehydrated and dripping with sweat, too shocked to speak. Scott had left us. It was Cordwell who first broke the silence.

'How fucking stupid.'

Brown and Avery had slumped down side by side on the concrete floor, with their backs against the rough plaster. White sat on the benches, in his grubby rugby shorts, with his head between his knees. Sweat ran off his forehead and dripped from his nose onto the floor.

Sampson, who was the only man still standing, said, 'I can't believe we've just done that.' He pulled off his T-shirt, saturated with perspiration, and threw it onto the floor. Wet and heavy, it made a loud clap on the concrete.

'I felt sure we would just go for a gentle jog,' I said.

'So did I.' Brown raised his head. Moisture flowed from his legs and onto the floor.

'It's stupid,' said Cordwell, 'what's the fucking point. Long Drag's on Friday night.'

'It's so you fail,' said Para.

Para took off his singlet and soaking shorts and walked over to the showers. One by one the seven of us followed him.

There were less than half a dozen jets that worked in the showers. Some were blocked, some had been snapped off, and one or two looked as though they had never worked. Hot water trickled out of a couple of jets and Para and Sampson vied for one of these ineffectual sprays. Fowkes found a fragment of soap on the tiles and used it to try to get a lather in his hair, but only cold water ran out of his shower, like the last few drops in a watering can.

'I got the sack on Friday,' said Para, soaping his body.

'You what?' said Cordwell, turning away from the wall.

'I got the sack. I asked for two weeks off to go away with the TA, and my boss said no.'

'What a bastard.'

'He said, "You've only just started. There's three million people unemployed out there. What would I do if every one of my employees went off to play soldiers every five minutes?"'

'What did you say?'

'Fuck you! And then I walked out. And then I had my fucking missis to contend with.'

'Come and work for me,' said Fowkes.

'It makes me sick,' said Cordwell, reaching for his towel. It hung from the chromium rail at the end of the showers. 'You work your bollocks off all week, rush all day Friday, get to the barracks, pack, thrash all the way up to North Wales, and then run all fucking night. We get two hours for breakfast and then we run all fucking day. Then it's PT. We battle back down the motorway for five or six hours and then wash the four-tonner. And then we have to clean our fucking kit. Last weekend I got eight hours' sleep in seventy-two hours, and when I walked into the office on Monday morning, the receptionist said, "Did you have a nice weekend?"'

THE PRIZE

*It is an appalling thing to feel all one possesses
drain away.*

Pascal

Is this really happening? Bed at two and up at four. Surely not. I feel
horribly sick.

'Ballinger. You've got twenty hours. Go.'

At last, motion. Anything is better than standing around. I can
see only one thing: a compass needle and a direction. It's pitch
black. If only it wasn't so cloudy. A moon, a few stars, anything
would be better than this.

'It's going to be as black as a witch's tit up there, lads.'

'Run, run, run.'

Don't stop. A bog . . . Go through it. You haven't got time to
waste. Stay on course. Watch the bearing. Nothing else is important.

Run.

Another hill. Come on. Attack it. Remember what Falstaff said:
'Climb it, spit on it, press on.'

Push it.

'It's your country, lads. Look after it. That's why you're here,
isn't it?'

'Aggression, lads. Speed and aggression . . . That's what it's all
about.'

'If you get blisters so fucking what? . . . It's only fucking pain

. . . Remember, lads, a day is but twenty-four hours long.'

'I've been on so many night marches, I've lost count.'

'What about kit?'

'Get the best.'

Come on. Keep it going. You're doing well.

Not another drystone wall. It looked miles away: a deception of the night. Come on, straight over . . . Now where? Must be that way.

Run.

You're going beautifully.

'You enjoying it, Avery?'

'Yes, staff. We going around Regent's Park next, staff?'

Keep going. Keep the rhythm. You're doing well.

'You. Yes you. You got a big dick or something?'

'He's ruthless. We save him for the new recruits. Scares the life out of them.'

'Wood, learn to write before next week.'

'Sir.'

The sky is changing rapidly. The clouds are rumbling forwards.

'This, lads, is a race. Just keep fucking going.'

'I want the best blokes first.'

'He doesn't think we're the best.'

'Of course he doesn't.'

Huge charcoal grey clouds tumble across the sky, like boulders thundering down a hillside.

'My wife does them in the winter. I frame them. Shockingly expensive to get them done . . . Marine Artists, but not much marine scenery here. Going far?'

'Now, I ask you, how can a man on forty quid a week afford to die? It's bloody disgraceful.'

'All over the world people think money, sir . . . Money very important, I know . . . Bangladesh, India, Pakistan . . . Very difficult countries.'

'I know Shakespeare. Very great Englishman. Listen . . . *Tempest*. You know Shakespeare?'

The sky is changing colour quickly now: the clouds have rolled on. It's a deep translucent blue.

Look, there's the pack, silhouettes on the skyline. You've caught them.

That must be the second RV ahead. Excellent. This is it.

Make sure you are all done up for the RV. Good. Nothing is hanging out of my pockets. Buttons done up? Yes. Cap-comforter straight? Yes, that's all right. Good. Map? Make sure the map is ready. Once more: where have I come from? where am I now? He's bound to ask me. Remember what Scott said, be aggressive. I must let him know I mean business.

Excellent. That's the second RV.

Run.

I can see now: it's light, but there's a ground mist. The grass is wet and slippery.

'Why did you come with me?'

'To travel with an honest man for the last time.'

'How did you know I was honest?'

'Your feet, sir.'

'Feet?'

'Every man on this course wears issued boots. Is that clear? . . . No man on this course has an advantage.'

'Sorry, I've run out of mediums.'

'My fucking feet don't hurt . . . My fucking feet don't hurt.'

Careful. Don't be pressurized. Get the bearing right. That's it. A barn. Check it again. Don't rush. It's not time wasted. Remember. Think.

'We'll win this one.'

Another hill.

Come on. Push it.

This can't be right: it's a vertical rock face.

'White, this is madness.'

I'm clinging to a sharp, jagged crag with my fingers. My weapon is across my chest, in the V of my arms. My bergen is sliding around on my back pulling me outwards. The drop is sheer: two hundred feet to the water at the bottom.

Pull yourself up.

Don't shake.

'Come on . . . We can't stay down here all fucking night.'

'The grass is lethal: it's razor-sharp.'

Steady.

Not far now. Get to that tree and you're all right.

'Do not fucking grunt . . . Ever heard cows going in for milking?
. . . Blisters! . . . Bloody blisters . . . Wasters . . . Bloody wasters.'

Just a bit more.

Pull.

Thank God for that. Now which way?

Check the map. A marshy plateau. A hundred and ten degrees.

Run.

Keep going. Keep the rhythm.

Another incline. Keep going. It's uphill. Climbing is easier. It doesn't jar.

Yes. That's better. I'm sweating but at least my knee is OK.

That must be the third RV down there. Same procedure: check your pockets, buttons, cap-comforter, map. Give him everything he wants . . .

'Aggression, lads . . . Speed and aggression, that's what it's all about.'

Good. That's the third RV. Fifteen hours to go. If only I knew how far it was.

My fucking knee. A change in pace is awful. It's downhill now – that's worse.

Come on.

My eyes water.

Run.

Water.

'It's going to be as dry as a witch's tit up there: the streams are empty.'

'I've got to get down to water.'

'Para's really struggling.'

'Is he?'

'He's run out of water.'

'Is there any water?'

'Yes, in the jerry cans, by the Storeman's four-tonner.'

Don't slow down.

Run.

Someone's twisting a knife in my knee. A recruit in Two Squadron overtakes me. He smiles. He thinks I'm down. I can see it in his eyes.

'What we want is lunatics . . . Speed and aggression.'

Dear God let it end. My lower leg hangs like a puppet from my knee. When I put my foot on the ground it crumples. I'm tired now. The pain is sapping me. Every step hurts.

Run, run.

'Ballinger!'

'Yes, staff?'

'What the fuck do you think you're doing?'

'Crossing the road, staff.'

'You're not. You're walking along the side of it. This regiment never uses roads, Ballinger.'

'I was just about to cross—'

'Get down there, Ballinger, and give me twenty. *Move!* Keep your bergen on.'

Where the fuck did he come from? It would have to be Scott, wouldn't it.

'*You!* That's not a fucking press-up . . . *Get down!* That's not a fucking press-up. Down. Up . . . Down, up.'

I can't do it. Four and a half stone slips around on my back. Why has it got to be in this ditch?

'Down, Ballinger. Get fucking down.

'OK. That'll do. Up you get. Start switching on, Ballinger. You've got some lost time to make up now. *Move!*'

'What we want is lunatics.'

'Fucking loved it. That's why I'm here.'

''Alf his head had gone.'

'Listen to your corporal. Every time you stop your senses should be tingling. Study your map, check your position, re-check it . . . When your corporal's talking to you, shut up and listen. One hundred per cent attention. Is that clear?'

'I'll be watching you.'

Get away from Scott – you must get away . . .

Try to run.

Don't wince.

Follow the drystone wall. Cling to it. It climbs up into the mist.

Come on – you must get away from him.

Run.

'Switch on, Ballinger.'

'It's a mental attitude.'

'You, Ballinger, have got to be a lot more aggressive . . . You're too fucking casual.'

'Why?'

'Thief, sir.'

'Thief!'

'One day, sir, you will buy a boat. You will be the captain and pull the string. I will work the engine and collect the money. Seventy-five per cent for you, twenty-five for me.'

Cordwell overtakes me on the mountainside, but then turns. He recognizes me in the fog. 'You all right?'

'Yes.'

'I'm all right. I went too fast at the beginning. I'm through. You go on. I'll be all right.'

'I can't make it. I'm going back to the barn.'

Cordwell speaks again, back through the swirling fog, 'It's not far to the RV. Keep going.'

'Now, lads, Selection really begins.'

'You blokes are deluding yourselves . . . Some of you are fucking hopeless . . . Run, run, run.'

Is that an RV or am I dreaming?

'This is not the fucking Girl Guides . . . You have got to dig in . . . It's a mental attitude.'

It's the fourth RV. Another grid reference.

Careful. Think.

Run.

My leg hangs loosely. Tie it. Bind it. Make it solid.

No. Don't stop.

'If you stop once, lads, you stop twice.'

'He makes it sound like a holiday for two in Paris.'

'Take it on the bone. On the bone. Muscle tires. Let it rest on the bone. In step. In step. Come on, boys . . . Catch those buggers.'

Think.

Run.

'If you want to go, sir, we will go . . . I'm not afraid. I'm not afraid to—'

'I am a Muslim man, sir. You cannot know about this . . . You don't know Bengali culture. I know Bengali mind, Bengali religion. I am a Muslim man, sir: I was born a Muslim man. I have Muslim blood in my body. You are a Christian man, sir: you have Christian body and Christian blood, Christian women, everything.'

'I am not afraid, sir.'

'God knows about everything.'

'It's been buggered up . . . All that life . . . Buggered up, I tell you. Disgraceful . . . Bloody disgraceful.'

I don't believe it. No. Not more clumpy moon grass.

The light is fading.

Sampson overtakes me. 'OK?'

Para follows a few minutes later. Sampson has already slipped into the mist. We grunt at each other.

Come on. Keep going. Get across this moon grass.

Forwards. Just go forwards.

'It's up to you, lads . . . You've got to fucking want it . . . You've got to fucking want it.'

It's getting darker. The mist is clearing. Soon there will be a North Star.

'Look at the colours.'

'You can't sit here all day.'

'Yes I can. Look at the colours.'

Chew air. Keep your face moving. Force your eyes open.

Run.

How much further? Keep on the compass bearing.

A track.

Stay on it. It's dark. It should go to the RV.

Crunch.

'Is that you, Brown?'

'Yes.'

'How far is it to the RV?'

'About forty minutes – straight up this track.'

Switch on.

No. Switch off: don't think.

'Fowkes? Is that you?'

'Yes.'

'I'm fucked. Both my knees have gone. I think I've torn a ligament.' Fowkes doesn't hear. He walks past me on into the night.

The North Star.

It's black but the light is still there.

Run.

An RV. A candle flickers on a Land Rover dashboard. It has nearly expired.

I cling to the wing mirror, and use it like a crutch. I knock on the window. My weapon is lying across my boot. That's allowed – only at RVs.

The window is dripping in condensation. It is wound down slowly.

Another grid reference.

How much more? It's at least six miles away and it's nine o'clock. There are only a few hours left.

'Careful!'

'Who's that?' I can see nothing except the night.

'I'm having a rest. You nearly stood on me.'

'Where are you?'

'Just in front of you. I'm lying down. I've got to have a sleep.'

A black form is slumped, like a drunken man, across the track.

'Just a short sleep.'

Run. Leave him alone.

Stabbing pains, as if there's a knife in my cartilages.

Is this the end?

'You've got to be a lot more aggressive, Ballinger.'

'Why?'

'Well done. Fucking well done. How are your feet?'

'I don't know, sir. I can't feel them. It's my knee. I think it's packed up.'

'There's not a man in this regiment who's not had injured knees.'

I smile, trying to give nothing away.

'Good effort,' the OC says. 'Get on the four-tonner and get yourself a brew.'

Two arms come down from the tail-gate in the darkness.

'Give us your kit, mate. Fucking good effort.'

Someone passes me a painkiller with a mug of soup.

'Here. Take this.'

'No, thanks.'

'Other blokes took them on the run.'

'Did they?'

Silence. I'm too tired to talk.

'How do you feel?'

'Terrible. How do I look?'

'Fucked.'

It was ten o'clock. I had been moving for just over sixteen hours without stopping for more than a few minutes. I faded in the corner of the four-tonner. Was this really the end or was I dreaming? Suppose this is not the end, but the end is really ten kilometres further on. I have to get up, and go on. Get up? I can't. I won't. I must. Is our ability to withstand pain inexhaustible? No. Yes. Of course it is. Go on. Keep moving. Don't go down yet. The end is not far now. Soon rest. Soon sleep. Run, run, run . . .

'OK, off you get, lads. Find yourself a basha site and get some kip.' The truck had taken us to another location but I was too tired to realize.

When I came to, recruits were still coming in. Avery smiled from the back of a four-tonner. He had made it with less than an hour to spare. White was helped off the ambulance: Falstaff was sorry to lose him.

'We need men like you badly,' he said, looking at White.

White was a good man. At the second RV the corporals would not let him go on. He had strained his groin too severely to be left alone on the hills. He had failed and the disappointment was written across his face.

'Tough shit, White. Life's a bitch.' Falstaff smiled, nothing seemed to perturb him. 'Shall we see you on the next course?'

US

A poor life this if, full of care,
We have no time to stand and stare.

W. H. Davies

On Sunday lunchtime two small buses, the kind the Gurkhas use, arrived at the basha site. The eight of us in One Squadron, together with Scott and the OC, climbed aboard. The recruits in the other squadrons climbed up into the second bus and sat with their corporals.

I had only one thought in my head and that was sleep.

Technically, there should have been an abundance of room, but by the time the back had been loaded with eight bergens and kit bags, eight weapons and Scott's and the OC's personal belongings, we were reduced to one double seat per man. And the seats were tiny.

They were basic, rigid, and firmly bolted to the floor. Each was rock hard, despite being covered in deceptive green plastic. All the corners were right-angles and the seats neither reclined nor moved. The ones in front were too close, like the benches in the upper circle of a Victorian theatre, and any movement between them was a struggle. Even the gangway was hopelessly narrow; so much so that Sampson could only just edge along it sideways.

For a man with damaged knees, who desires nothing more than to stretch out his legs, a Gurkha bus is the worst of all possible conveyances. A donkey would be more comfortable, for then one's legs could dangle freely, and one would not have to force a bend, repeatedly, at the knees.

'If only we were in a four-tonner,' said Fowkes. 'Funny,' he continued, 'I never thought I'd say that.'

White sat on his own, on the seat immediately behind the driver. Scott sat opposite him, on the other side of the gangway. Then there were two or three empty rows before the rest of us. We sat, more or less together, on separate seats. We tried, where possible, to lean across the seats with our feet up and our backs against the windows, struggling for a few minutes of comfort.

The lean OC perched bird-like on the edge of his seat, in the middle of us. As we drove through a housing estate, following signs for a motorway, he began the conversation.

'You did well, lads. I'm pleased – very pleased. You've lost one,' he said, looking over the tops of the seats towards White. But White was swaying in sleep.

'How far was it, sir?' Avery asked.

'Between sixty and sixty-five kilometres, depending on the route you took. The shortest possible distance was just over sixty.

'I always say, lads, Long Drag is a landmark in a man's life. You're still only a third of the way through the course, but it's Long Drag that makes a man. Even TQ is different. When a man gets through Long Drag, I respect him. I always listen to what he has to say, even if he goes on to fail the course.'

'What do you do with all the figures the PSI keeps, sir?' I asked, shuffling awkwardly in my seat.

'They're all stored. Every question, every error, everything. It all goes down against you, lads. Nothing is forgotten.'

I looked at Avery and we both smiled.

'When people ask you what you do, sir, what do you say?' I asked again.

'I say I'm in the TA.'

'But what unit, sir?' Avery asked.

'Anything but this unit. Choose an infantry regiment if you like – anything but this one.

'How did you find the course?' the OC asked, posing a general question.

'Tough,' said Avery.

'It's hard to do anything else,' I said, 'when you're doing this.'

'Good. That's as it should be. It takes a hundred per cent, lads, nothing less. It's about priorities, lads. You're going to face difficult choices at times, if you haven't already. I'm a solicitor in civilian life. I came up here on Thursday to get this weekend organized. I take a lot of Fridays off. It's not easy, but,' he said, grinning, 'my partners know me by now.

'I've given eighteen years to this regiment and I've a wife and two kids at home. They're hard decisions, lads, but you've got to face them. When I did Selection, nothing was going to stop me, and that was the same for the next fourteen or fifteen years. Only now, in the last year or two, have I started to put my kids first. You've probably noticed that at the end of a weekend I'm the first to leave. I leave the admin to the corporals now.'

'How old are your kids, sir?' Fowkes asked.

'My son's nine and my daughter's seven.

'You've got to get your priorities sorted out, lads. You shouldn't be thinking about marriage at this stage. How old are you?'

'I'm twenty-one, sir.'

'I'm twenty-seven, sir.'

'Twenty-six.'

'Twenty-eight, sir.'

'Twenty-five.'

'There you are then. Most blokes in this regiment put in at least six weeks a year on full-time courses in their first two or three years. And that's in addition to the regimental exercises. You've got to get the basics under your belts, lads. You blokes should be thinking in terms of a minimum of three years. That's what it takes, just to get accepted by this regiment.'

Cordwell, sitting behind me, murmured, 'I can't do that. I don't get six weeks' holiday a year.'

It started to rain, and the driver switched on the wipers. We had

left the housing estate and were on an open road. The fields
stretched out to a treeline in the distance.

'What did you think of the course, sir?' Avery asked. 'Do they
follow a pattern?'

'Good question. Yes, they do. Weekend four always sorts out
the wishful-thinkers and the no-hopers, but your course was
unusual: it was fucking decimated. I didn't expect that. We're
going to introduce milling on the next course. It's not our style.
They do it in the Paras, but it does sort out the men who aren't
aggressive enough. It's good: it teaches you not to be afraid of men.'

'What is it?' I asked.

Para and Fowkes laughed.

'Don't laugh,' said the OC.

'Sixty seconds on a concrete floor,' said Fowkes, 'to beat up your
opponent.'

'It's good for aggression, lads. But it's not a spectator sport. Even
badged members of this regiment will not be allowed to watch.
And it's good for resistance to interrogation.'

It started to rain more heavily and the raindrops streaked, like
snail trails, across the glass.

'Thank God we didn't have to do that,' said Cordwell when the
OC was not listening. 'I couldn't go into a client meeting on
Monday morning with a broken nose. You can say what you like,
no one would fucking believe you.'

For a long while no one said anything. The OC sat back in his
seat, picked up his file and started to sort out his papers. Fowkes
stretched out sideways on the floor of the bus and tried to sleep
between the rows of seats. I put my jacket behind my back and up
against the window. Through the driving rain I could see a sign in
the dusk that said, 'M1 5 miles'.

I must have slept for several hours. It was the hailstones that woke
me, pinging against the window pane. The conversation appeared
to go on between whoever was awake.

Avery and Cordwell were talking to the OC. Brown was fast
asleep, twisted like a contortionist on the green plastic.

'Your PSI is not like some we get,' the OC said. 'Some of them have got no time for the TA, but yours is excellent. You heard him on the first weekend. He said, "For the next year I'm attached to 21 SAS." He said it with pride, lads. And he meant it. They're not all like that in 22. He's fucking good.'

An hour or so later Fowkes got up from the floor and joined in the conversation. 'Para's lost his job, sir, because of this.'

'Did he?' But the OC seemed neither surprised nor interested. Later on he said, 'If I interview two blokes for a job, and they're exactly the same in all other respects, I'll always give the job to the one who's been in the TA. It doesn't matter what unit. It shows he's got a bit more, done something else.'

I fell asleep again and when I woke we were somewhere near Northampton. We had slowed down to about twenty miles per hour: all three lanes of the motorway were solid with traffic. It was dark and the wipers swung back and forth monotonously across the windscreen.

'Well, we've made it so far,' said Brown, waking up. 'That's the first major hurdle over. I couldn't go back to our old unit now, could you?'

'Fuck no,' said Avery.

'It just wouldn't be the same.'

'No. They've got no fucking idea.'

'You did well to avoid Scott,' I said. 'He found me. I felt sure he'd try to find you and wear you down.'

'That's the one thing that kept me going,' said Avery. 'It was the thought of Scott thinking I'd failed. Nothing was going to fucking stop me. I'd have crawled if I had to.'

We drove on past the M25. The glare of the headlights glistened in the rain. White lay with his head resting against the window. 'Leave him alone,' said Cordwell. 'He's probably asleep.'

'Camp on Friday, lads,' the OC said. 'You'll need a different sort of fitness. The Paras among you will know what I mean. You've got to carry your injuries on Camp. I don't want to see any fucking whingers. Have a rest this week, lads. Just think, you'll be up to your thighs in flesh tonight.'

As we turned into the barracks the rain, shimmering in the dim street lights, eased to a steady drizzle.

'I shall see you lot on Friday,' the OC said, clutching his file and standing up.

We threw the luggage out of the emergency door at the back of the bus, and onto the barrack-square below. White handed his kit back to the Storeman and, seeing us, forced a smile. He shouldered his civilian sports bag and walked out of the barracks alone.

HOLIDAYS

He felt terribly embarrassed: they were all dressed and he was undressed and, strange to say, without clothes he seemed to feel guilty in their presence and, what was worse, he was almost convinced himself that he really was inferior to them all and now they were fully entitled to despise him.

Dostoyevsky

'I can see you've done this before.' The Storeman gave me a surly glance.

'Not at all. This is my first time.'

'CCF? OTC? You have some experience?'

'None, I'm afraid. I'm a civilian.'

'Boy Scouts?'

'Yes,' I said.

'For how long?'

Standing in the armoury I tried to find the date of my investiture in the back of my mind. 'About ten years.'

'Thought so. I can always tell. All the best blokes were in the Boy Scouts.'

The Storeman laid my SA80 on the counter and made a note of the serial number in his logbook. He also passed me four empty magazines capable of holding thirty rounds each.

'Look after these,' he said, laying them beside the weapon. 'If you don't keep them clean, they'll jam and then you'll look a right cunt.'

Outside, on the barrack-square the other six members of One Squadron stood around their bulging bergens and full kit bags. Para had brought three pairs of boots; one for wearing during the day and two perfectly polished pairs, to be reserved for parade and inspection. Even Sampson, the only other civilian, had managed to acquire a spare pair of boots. Extra pairs were allowed on Camp. I was alone, however, in having the bare minimum and nothing more than the issued kit.

Each man held his weapon in his right or left hand and had dumped his webbing, together with the magazines, on top of his pile of belongings.

The OC entered the barracks and walked across the square towards us. He came wearing a grey single-breasted suit and carrying an angular, brown leather briefcase.

'All set, lads?' he said, coming up to us.

'Yes, sir,' said several voices together.

'Good.' He looked keenly at our bergens. 'That's your house, lads, for the next two weeks. Keep it in good order. Is Corporal Scott here yet?'

'He's gone to see the Storeman, sir,' said Avery.

'Good. The transport should be here soon. It's going to be a long journey tonight.'

'Where're we going, sir?' Avery asked.

'Scotland. We'll be joining up with 23 SAS for the next two weeks. They've just done Long Drag too. A word of warning though. There's some fucking fit blokes in 23. They train in the Cairngorms. I'll be splitting you up on Camp: you won't all be together, you'll be divided into sections. Don't worry, you'll soon get to know some of them, lads. They've got some good blokes.'

'What's Camp like, sir?' It was dusk and Fowkes stood in his charcoal grey suit, casually holding his weapon in his right hand. His white cotton shirt was noticeably creased and his blue silk tie was stained with gun oil.

'Wait and see,' said the OC. 'Camp's going to be a bit different. I shouldn't be telling you this, it's not fair on the other squadrons. Camp's about working in a team. You've proved you can carry a bergen over the hills, but that's all. Over the next two weeks, I shall be watching each one of you to see if you can work in a patrol. But I warn you, if I see anyone fucking about, or with the wrong attitude, he's off the course. For the civvies among you, that means you're back on the streets. Some blokes think that because they've passed Long Drag they can ease off. You give it one hundred per cent, lads, all the fucking time. You'll be watched twenty-four hours a day, every day. You're a long way from the end yet, don't forget that.'

'Is the PSI coming, sir?' Avery asked.

'Yes. There's going to be strong presence from 22. Your PSI for Continuation will also be there. He's taking over after Camp and he'll be watching you very closely.'

'What's he like, sir?' Fowkes asked.

The OC smiled and started nodding very slightly, as was his tendency when he got excited. 'Wait and see, lads. Wait and see.'

'Do we go through interrogation on Camp, sir?' Fowkes continued.

'Yes. But it's called TQ, Tactical Questioning. If you fail it, and a lot of blokes do, that's it. A pity when you've gone through Long Drag, but you've got to think. You've got to use the grey matter.

'Here comes Corporal Scott,' he said, looking across the parade-ground. 'I'll see you later. I've got to get my papers. Tell him the bus is due in half an hour.'

Scott walked over to us and tried to join the conversation but no one was inclined to include him. After several false starts he turned away and began to go through his civilian bag. He pulled out a magazine with a picture of an armed frogman on the front, sat on his bergen, and began to read.

I turned to Brown and said, 'Did you bring a book with you?'

'You've got to be bloody joking,' said Cordwell, turning round and speaking before Brown. 'You won't even have time to piss in the next two weeks.'

'Did you go through interrogation in your old unit?' I asked Brown when Cordwell had finished.

'Yes,' said Brown, 'but I doubt if it will be anything like this.'

Brown stood in his plain grey suit and immaculately polished, black leather shoes. The soles were made of soft rubber. Under his jacket he wore a green striped shirt and rectangular cuff-links. The silver, which was just visible when he moved his arms, shone in the setting sun.

'We did a short Resistance to Interrogation course, but Avery escaped. We were set against an infantry unit in the regular army. They caught Avery and me, and threw us into the back of a personnel carrier.'

'Were you blindfolded?'

'Yes. But Avery managed to open the back and jump out. He thought we were going about ten miles an hour. When we stopped they couldn't work out what had happened to him. They couldn't believe he'd jumped: we were doing forty miles an hour.'

'Was he injured?'

'Not really.'

'What's this I hear,' I said, calling across to Avery, 'about you jumping from a personnel carrier?'

Avery swung round, left Sampson and Fowkes, and strode over. He had come straight from work and he was still wearing his navy pin-stripes and a pair of black Oxfords, the heels built up with metal wedges. When he walked the steel bit into the gravel.

'Bloody painful,' he said. 'I thought it was only doing about ten miles an hour. Still, they left me alone after that.'

'Can we escape during our exercise?' I asked.

'No,' said Brown. 'It's a test. You've got to survive it. The interrogation is the least of it, that's just the questioning. It's the build-up that's the worst part.'

'They'll rough you up a bit,' said Avery, smiling. 'A lot of shouting. They try to frighten you. It's usually about eight hours' build-up followed by two hours' TQ, but I don't know with these people. They may do sixteen hours, and then four, or it might even be twenty-four hours' build-up.'

'It's very controlled,' said Brown. 'It has to be supervised by a medic. They just try to humiliate you.'

'Just?'

The OC came back out clutching his file of waterproofed papers and guessed what we were talking about. 'When I did TQ we were set against the Paras. 'Course they fucking loved it. It was a feather in the cap for them. The whole thing degenerated into a fucking big punch-up. One bloke was coughing up blood for two days afterwards. It's a real experience, lads. You're privileged,' he said, turning to Avery who had begun to laugh. 'You can't do this in the regular army: it's Special Forces only.'

The following morning we woke in a long dormitory, like a hospital ward, with the beds pushed up against the two parallel walls. The beds were made of steel tubing with a base of strung wire. Sealed green plastic, for ease of washing, encased the foam mattresses. A long, thin gangway, its yellow floor tiles scuffed black with army boots, separated the rows of beds. Groups of slender lockers clustered around the door.

An archway divided the dormitory in two. I was in the first of these halves, known as Room One. In our room, moulded plastic chairs and small Formica-topped tables alternated between the beds. They served to keep each one about two feet from the next. Above my bed was a small window, and a pair of pale blue curtains hung from a rusty metal rail. I was next to Brown and opposite me was Fowkes. In the second half, known as Room Two, Avery, Cordwell, Para and Sampson found beds close together. Recruits from the other squadrons in 21 SAS, and from 23 SAS, occupied the remaining beds.

The dormitory was one room in a large purpose-built block, and our building was one of a multitude. The sparse and sprawling barracks extended for a mile or more into the surrounding hills, before being checked by a fence topped with razor wire. Electronic beams flashed across the ground, just outside the perimeter fencing, providing another security screen.

After a sloppy breakfast in a room known as the cookhouse, we filed into a dull hall, rather grandly called a lecture theatre, where the OC was waiting for us on a small platform at the front.

'Welcome to Camp, lads,' he said, his head ticking very slightly with excitement. 'You've made it, so far. We have fifty-four recruits with us from 21 and 23 SAS. Nine of you have no previous military experience. 21 is the sponsor of this Camp and I'm the officer in charge. I'm attached to One Squadron in that regiment.

'I have split you into nine sections of six and, for the next two weeks, you will do almost everything in these sections. I've got your allocation numbers here, so listen in for your name and section number.'

He ran through the list of recruits, calling out a number between one and nine for each man. He put Brown, Para and me together in Section Three. He put Avery and Sampson in Section Two, Fowkes in Section One and Cordwell in Section Five. When he had finished calling out the names and numbers he concluded his brief for Camp.

'One more thing, lads,' he said, 'for the next two weeks, walking is forbidden. I do not want to see anyone nonchalantly strolling about. You fucking run. OK, form up in your sections outside. Your corporals will give you the brief for the rest of the day.'

We gathered outside in our new sections. The other members of Section Three were Heel, who was in his thirties and had served with a regular infantry unit, and was now a welder; Ham, who was a civilian in Manchester; and McNeil, who was a Topographical Science undergraduate. All three were trying to join 23 SAS.

Scott was put in charge of Section Two, overseeing Avery and Sampson. The OC put us in the care of Corporal Spike. I had met him before, during Selection. He was in 21 SAS but in one of the other squadrons, and had occasionally manned an RV. He was stocky, firm and well built. If anything, he was unusually heavy for the SAS. He was not memorably fit. He excused himself from most forms of exercise by claiming a parachute injury. If there was an easy way of doing something, Spike would do it. He would climb a gate, rather than straddle a barbed-wire fence noisily and risk injury. His night sight was remarkable but in daylight his eyes were not penetrating. His hair gave his character away. It was ginger, cut short and inconsistently combed.

That evening, after a day practising our weapons drills, Brown,

Para and I sat together for dinner in the cookhouse. The members of the regiment sat at a special reserved table, masters in their own school.

'At least we're not on guard duty tonight,' said Brown.

'Our turn will come,' said Para, cutting into a fatty piece of roast pork.

'What does it involve?' I asked.

'Staying awake all fucking night,' said Para.

'You've got to patrol the fence and man the gatehouse,' said Brown. 'I expect they take it in turns.'

'You do it in pairs,' said Para, spitting out a piece of gristle. 'One pair sleeps while another walks about. The other does the gate-house. You swap round every hour or so. It's fucking boring.'

'You've got to have someone up through the night,' said Brown. 'It's in case there're any terrorist attacks. The IRA tried to bomb the Paras' barracks quite recently.'

'Yes, but they were fucking spotted,' said Para.

Spike woke us for PT which consisted of a four-mile run, in twenty-five minutes, in boots and over rough, hilly ground. Many of us still carried injuries sustained on Long Drag, but fortunately it was dark so our winces and hobbles were not noticed by the OC.

Fifteen minutes was allocated to shave, shower, clean one's boots, dress for parade and eat breakfast. Breakfast, which consisted of cornflakes with powdered milk and a fried egg, was, conse-quently, a miserable affair. I tried to force it all down within a minute or two, but it was not easy; chewing is so time-consuming.

After parade, and the brief for the day, we climbed with Section Four into the back of a four-tonner and lurched out of the barracks. We drove, in convoy, for forty minutes through the Scottish Lowlands. Soft, muddy fields rose and fell like a smooth swell in the sea. Brown slumped in the corner and slept for the duration of the journey. Para smoked.

We came to rest just over a cattle-grid at the foot of a firing range with eighteen targets. Sections Four, Five and Six doubled down to the butts. We, in the first three sections, lined up in front of the targets at the one-hundred-yard mark. Sections Seven to Nine jogged to a parallel range.

Several instructors paced around. Falstaff stood with a pair of ear defenders in one hand and an old-fashioned, portable box telephone in the other. The OC danced about excitedly, like a blackbird springing across a lawn, looking for prey.

The Storeman gave fifty live rounds to each man and we loaded our magazines. Section One took the first six targets, Section Two the second six and Section Three the remainder. Avery stood to my left and Para to my right. Brown was beyond Para.

'Remember everything you've been taught,' said Scott unnecessarily, encroaching on our section.

Falstaff shouted into his telephone and the instructor supervising the activity in the butts hoisted the red range flag.

Falstaff called out the instructions. We were to fire five rounds in our own time, unload our weapons and stand up when we had finished. When every man had fired we would run, as a group, down the range and examine our targets. We would assess our scores and, if necessary, calibrate our sights. We were to repeat this with another five rounds to check the settings. The remaining forty rounds were to be fired as four sets of ten; one set at each of the lines at one, two, three and four hundred yards. The scores would be recorded.

Falstaff bellowed out the commands across the wide range. '*Prone position.*

'*Load.*

'*In your own time, five rounds, fire!*'

Eighteen SA80s shattered the silence.

When I had finished I stood up and took one step backwards. Avery and a number of others were already standing. After several minutes only Para lay on the gravel, squeezing himself up tightly against the sandbag. He lay rigid, his weapon clamped in a vice-like grip. The barrel rose and fell with his smooth, controlled breathing. And then, at his leisure, he stopped the passage of air, and the barrel lay motionless like a corpse. Very gently, he took up the slack in the trigger and then squeezed. An empty cartridge shot through the air towards Brown, the brass flashing in the sun. It was the only perceptible movement. Para eased the trigger back, and lowered the weapon. Looking over the optics he rested his eyes and exhaled. A thread of smoke curled upwards from the mouth of the barrel and disappeared, like warm, colourless vapour in the sharp, autumnal air. There was silence again.

Avery and I looked at each other and Avery raised an eyebrow. When Para had unloaded his weapon, he stood up and we all ran forwards to our targets.

The targets had been lowered by the men in the butts and they were busy circling the perforations with coloured chalk. As we approached, they hoisted the targets again and we examined our scores. Most of us in One Squadron were more interested in Para's performance than our own. His accuracy was impressive but only marginally better than Avery's.

Later, when we moved back to the four-hundred-yard mark, I lay in the prone position looking at the target. It was crystal clear through my optic sights. I sent ten rounds out of ten through a man's chest, each within half an inch or so of the previous one. I was delighted, but the OC, who was watching my performance, was not congratulatory.

'Don't get too despondent,' he said, looking downcast. 'We all improve with time. In this regiment you've got to shoot a fly off a dog's bollocks at four hundred yards.'

Lunch, which was a ladle full of mutton stew, came round like meals on wheels in a Land Rover and we ate from our mess tins, languishing in the sun. When we had finished, we swapped with the second three sections. They used the range and we manned the butts.

At four o'clock the OC sent the four-tonners back to the barracks without us. We formed up on the edge of the range in eighteen rows of three, behind a tall man with a round face. He appeared to know Falstaff well, for they were often talking and laughing together. But in stature he could not have been more different. He was well over six feet tall and he carried no surplus weight. He wore a short-sleeved camouflaged shirt to match his trousers and bashed but polished boots. He did not wear a belt. He was a big man but not as obviously muscled as Sampson. His hair was thinning, and, on the crown of his head, he was starting to go bald. He said nothing. The OC gave the orders.

The tall man set the pace and we ran behind him. I was in the second rank with Heel and Brown. Cordwell and Fowkes were in the first.

It was eight kilometres to Camp and the tall man set a punishing pace for forty-five minutes. The sun shone relentlessly. As we ran I began to fall apart, like an overloaded suitcase that splits at the seams and starts shedding its load. My combat trousers slipped to beyond my hips so that the crotch was at my knees, and my webbing jumped all over the place. The pockets of my combat jacket were, as always, hopelessly overfull and uncomfortable. I unzipped the front so that my chest was bare, but then the jacket flapped irritatingly. All the time, our pace-maker ran effortlessly ahead. Occasionally he would turn to check that we were still with him. He must have been disappointed, for the line stretched out for nearly a mile. His age was deceptive: this man sprang through the Lowlands like a young roe.

I was near the front and, luckily, escaped the abuse levelled at those further back.

'You! What's your name?' a voice screamed ten yards behind me.

'Rose, sir.'

'What's your surname?' But the officer in 23 didn't wait for an answer.

'Make way, wimps, for the hard men,' grunted Scott when he found a man slowing down.

Back in the dormitory and streaming with sweat, I sat on my bed and looked at Brown. 'Who was that who led the run?' I asked.

'Search me,' said Brown. 'Ask Para.'

'That's Birch,' said Para, when I asked him later in the showers. 'He's the PSI for Continuation. He'll be with us now until the end of the course.'

'How old is he?'

'About forty, I think.'

A loud electronic alarm woke us. It was Heel's radio alarm. He got up first and shaved in approximately forty seconds by being brutal with his razor blade. The rest of us came to our senses slowly as Radio North disturbed our tranquillity.

There was no PT, which was a bad omen. I washed, shaved and then got dressed. Brown got dressed, even to the extent of fully lacing his boots, and then washed. We made our beds and cleaned our boots. One had to be meticulous in both of these. Heel did guard duty one night because his pillow was not straight.

That morning we drove to a new training area. The four-tonners stopped on the rim of a sweeping, elliptical depression about two miles wide and five miles long. Tank tracks cut cleanly through the uneven basin, slashing the green fields so that the wet mud oozed like blood in a wound. Naked fir trees, fighting for light, stood checked and huddled together, their clumps interspersed with solitary oaks, stripped and blackened by lightning.

Grass grew on the steep hillsides and a few deciduous trees divided what were once acres of pasture. A chestnut wood dropped away from the four-tonners and stopped at the marshy ground at the bottom. A few tributaries trickled down the incline and flowed into the stream saturating the lowest ground. A stark quarry had been blasted out of the slope on the far side of the depression leaving a network of twisting tracks, tangled with the spoil.

The metal casings of spent explosives littered the countryside. Cartridge cases that had not been collected lay trodden into the leaves alongside empty acorn cups.

Small displays had been set up around the training ground. All day we rotated in our sections from one to the other, taking our notebooks with us. At each stand we were given a different lecture. One was entitled 'Fieldcraft', another 'The Different Methods of Judging Distances', and another 'The Art of Concealment'. During one lecture we were shown how to describe the scene in front of us, using reference points, angles and an agreed terminology.

We were taught perspective, to train our eyes and search for a focal point. We had to scan the landscape and pick out the dominant features, just as an artist would peer ever deeper trying to unravel colours. Like the painter who is restricted by the size of his canvas, we were constrained by our arcs of reference. We were also instructed in interpretation: countryside became terrain, rolling hills became gradients that slow down one's progress across country, wild hedgerows became areas of camouflage, mountain streams became obstacles and sources of water.

At the end of our lessons we formed up, once again, behind Birch and he paced us back to camp. We ran in combat uniform, helmet and boots. It was an eight-mile run, called a CFT or Combat Fitness Training. We carried our SA80s and put our webbing into our bergens so that the packs weighed nearly forty pounds. The basic infantry test allowed one hour forty minutes for this run. We sprinted round, trying in vain to ignore discomfort, in one hour ten minutes. Heel and I were in the front pack. Not at the front where we would have been noticed, but in the third rank keeping our heads straight. Ham ran alongside us and, as he struggled to keep up, we kept urging him to stay in step. Brown dropped, despite encouragement, further and further behind. Mucus swung from his nose, and sweat and phlegm dripped hideously from his chin.

Back in the dormitory, Brown slouched on the edge of his bed with his shoulders bent forwards towards the floor. He raised his head, but still keeping his eyes from me, said, 'The CFT changed me. It's the worst thing I've ever done.'

'What about Long Drag?' I asked, sitting up on my bed.

'Oh, that was OK. The CFT was worse, a lot worse. Something happened inside me. I don't know what it was.' He heaved a sigh before carrying on. 'I couldn't do anything. Everyone was overtaking me. I kept slipping back and then Scott looked across at me. He just looked; he didn't say anything. It was awful. It was his eyes. There was something about them that really frightened me.'

The following morning we walked – unusually – to the range for shooting practice. A farmer, however, was struggling behind the range to control a fire. And since stray bullets were deemed likely, shooting was cancelled and we doubled back to camp.

Brown and I quickly procured a tea urn from the cookhouse. Everyone was delighted. We sat out of sight in the courtyard in the middle of our dormitory building. The sun shone and we took off our helmets. A few recruits slept, some smoked and one or two were content to daydream. I scribbled in my notebook, until Scott arrived and our rest was over with a scream.

That night it was our turn to do guard duty. It was a night of no real sleep. First we had to patrol the fencing for an hour. Then we slept for an hour. Then Spike woke us and we had to man the gatehouse for an hour before going back on patrol again. The cycle repeated itself all night. We saw nothing remotely interesting, although vehicles passed through the gate several times an hour. All the occupants of every one had to be challenged.

During the night, when Ham and I should have been sleeping, Spike fried some bacon and made us sandwiches. When we sat down to eat he asked us about our motives for joining the regiment. Spike began by confessing his fear of being 'called up'. He would flee, he said, along with some of the others, to Tenerife, out of sight and sound of the telephone.

'Why did you join?' he asked me.

'It's a long story really,' I said.

I sat on board an old paddle-steamer that used to belong to the Governor of Bengal. It fell, on Partition, to East Pakistan and is permanently moored on the outskirts of Dhaka, a relic, a rotting carcass left to bask in the sun. It is now a floating restaurant, but is usually quiet.

I sat at a square table with a stained and torn linen cloth. Sitting opposite me was a small-framed Bengali who spoke English. As I watched the cargo boats glide smoothly downstream, I explained my plan.

I wanted to sail down the Padma River on a small boat and explore the Mouths of the Ganges, and, in particular, the Sundarbans.

And afterwards, if it was humanly possible, I wanted to trek in the Hill Tracts and meet a people who were part Burmese.

I had been to Burma, two years before, and found the visa restrictions frustrating. On this side of the border, I reasoned, I could travel for as long as I wished, in a little-known part of the world. I would be unlikely to meet other Europeans and so could satisfy a craving for adventure. I knew it would be dangerous; a country struggling to feed its people is always precarious, but, inexplicably, this added to the attraction.

Even the little man opposite me looked doubtful. He fingered his chipped tea cup and looked apprehensively at the river, and the slow-moving traffic.

I wanted him to come with me. I could not hope to succeed without a guide. I knew it would mean a separation, for him, from his wife and daughter, but not I hoped for long. We would occasionally return to Dhaka.

'It is possible, sir,' Hassan said. 'But first, I must try alone. If the boatman sees you he will ask a very expensive price.'

A waiter hovered around our table, but when I did not respond he moved to another. He sat down and started to finger a sugar bowl.

'Where did you learn your English?' I asked, looking at Hassan.

'After Liberation, sir.' And then there was a long pause. He stared into his tea cup and I turned my gaze away from him. 'I met an Englishman,' he continued. 'He was a very good man; a very kind man. He gave me food.'

'How did you meet him?'

'He was working on an American aid project. I came to Dhaka after Liberation. I had to. I was eleven years old: I had nothing.'

'Did you lose your family?'

'Yes,' Hassan said. 'They all died, except my uncle. The army: they killed them.

'I had no food for ten days,' he said, steering the conversation away from his family. 'I worked for ten days carrying oil, but my boss would not pay me until after ten days.'

'How did you live?'

'I drank water, sir, dirty water, for my body. Then I met the Englishman. He gave me no money, but every day he gave me food. I stayed with him for three years. He became my second father. He was a good man, sir, a very kind man. He taught me English.'

'You speak it very well,' I said. 'Why did you leave him?'

'He retired at sixty-five and returned to England. He said he would leave me one-quarter of his money when he dies.'

'Have you heard from him?'

'No, sir. I think he is dead now. I think his children have forgotten his promise.'

I moved in my chair and asked, 'What did you do when he left?'

'I went to India, sir. He gave me one hundred pounds to travel for six months. But,' he added proudly, 'I travelled for eighteen.'

'Why did you come back at all?'

'Because, sir, Bangladesh is my country. I am a Muslim man. You cannot know about this, you are a Christian man. Traveller has many lives, but I have only one life.'

'I went trekking in Bangladesh,' I said, looking down at my bacon sandwich. My hands were still oily and they discoloured the white bread. 'When I came back I went walking in the Pennines. I met a man who gave me the phone number.'

'Was he in 21?' Spike looked at me expectantly. A magazine of live rounds lay at arm's length, ready to be loaded.

'I don't think so. I think he was in 22.'

'Did he say he was?'

'No.'

'What about you, Ham?' Spike asked.

Ham looked up. A long slice of fatty bacon had slipped from his sandwich and he was trying to rescue it with his mouth. Ketchup ran over his dirty fingernails.

'I like the outdoors,' he said. 'I like caving and abseiling, but I can't afford to do them any more. I'd like to learn to parachute and freefall.'

*

At six o'clock in the morning the guard was relieved and the six of us doubled back to the dormitory to dress for parade. Scott came in looking even more restless than usual but he said nothing. The skin on the tops of his cheeks had a pale yellow tinge and his face looked blotchy.

'He's been beaten up,' said Para, when he had left again.

'How do you know?'

'It's fucking obvious. I bet he had a scrap with one of the 23 corporals. They can't stand him. I'm fucking glad he's not in charge of our section.'

We spent all day on the ranges. In the morning the first three sections practised firing whilst the second three manned the butts. The remaining three drove to another range. After lunch we swapped around. All of us in One Squadron, except Cordwell, were in the first three sections and, when in the butts, we looked after one target each. I stood between Avery and Brown. Para was to Brown's right. Fowkes and Sampson were at the far end looking after targets 1 and 2.

The telephone at the end of the butts crackled and the instructor hoisted the flag. We raised our targets and suddenly rounds rocketed down the range. Some ricocheted off the tops of the butts and stones and soil flew down in front of us. The rounds shot through the targets and drilled straight into the gravel embankment about twenty yards off. Grit and dust burst into the air as eighteen men punctured their cardboard figures, time and time again.

'Shit!' said Avery, when a round grazed the steel support of his target, showering him with metal dust. Automatic fire continued to slash the silence, and the gravel on the embankment jerked and heaved.

'Wouldn't like to be out there,' said Brown, shouting to me above the noise. 'Makes you realize what it would be like to be under heavy fire.'

'You'd have no fucking chance,' said Avery, taking out his ear plugs.

Gradually the noise died down until only one or two men fired off their last few rounds, like snipers keeping us alert. Gravel dust drifted through the air like tobacco smoke. When the command came, we lowered the perforated men, made a note of the scores, patched up the holes with sticky paper and raised them again. Almost instantly the crack of live fire cut through our conversation.

'What do you think of Birch, then?' I asked Avery. Avery's ear plugs were black with gun oil where he had been rolling them between his greasy fingers.

'He's bloody fit,' said Avery, 'I know that much.'

'Yes,' I said, 'but don't you think he's different?'

'I know what you mean,' said Brown. For once, Brown was smiling. He seemed to enjoy being in the butts. We were out of sight of Scott, Spike and the OC. With the exception of the one instructor in the butts, all members of the regiment stayed behind the firing line, supervising and watching every recruit. As long as the targets rose and fell, and were patched up in between, nobody seemed to care what happened at the end of the range. To that extent, the butts were more restful than the dormitory.

'He's different from the others all right,' said Brown, shouting above the bursts of fire. 'But I can't quite put my finger on it.'

'He's probably an officer,' said Avery. 'He sounds as though he's been in the Guards.'

'Para thinks he's about forty,' I said.

A round glanced off the steel frame bordering Brown's target and he instinctively ducked. Avery laughed. The firing continued and handfuls of gravel flew up at random into the air. Then the grit higher up the incline would slip, like dry sand, to fill the gaping depression.

'He doesn't say much,' I said.

'No, he doesn't,' said Brown, picking up his small box of sticky paper. 'He doesn't have to.'

When we were finally stood down for the day, at about eleven o'clock, five or six of us returned to our dormitory. The rest went to the naafi. Fowkes undressed quickly and threw his damp clothes in a heap at the bottom of his locker. Without shutting the door, he slipped into his narrow bed, wearing a grubby T-shirt and a pair of underpants.

I sat on the plastic chair dividing my bed from Brown's and started to unlace my boots. Brown sat on his bed, propped up by his pillow, with his legs stretched out in front of him. He wore a pale blue nylon T-shirt, that he saved for PT, and camouflaged trousers. He kept his boots on.

'Cheer up, Brown,' said Fowkes, looking across the gangway with his head resting on his pillow. He had pulled the white sheet and the two coarse blankets up to his chest. 'We're half-way through the first week already. Get through TQ next week and that's the end of Camp.'

'Yes,' said Brown, expressionless. He had scored fourteen out of twenty on that evening's night shoot, the product, he claimed, of pure chance: he couldn't see the target. One man had scored zero, and another twenty-one out of twenty: someone else had accidentally shot at his target.

'You don't look as though you're enjoying yourself,' I said, sitting up.

'I'm not,' said Brown. 'I hate these camps.'

'Why do you do it then?' I asked.

'I don't know. I suppose it's to prove myself, to win respect.'

'But that's ridiculous,' I said, 'especially if you don't even like it. Suppose you pass, then what?'

'I don't know.'

For a while Brown stared at his boots and said nothing. Fowkes had closed his eyes. In the adjoining room Cordwell and Para sat on Para's bed sharing out cigarettes.

'I'd like to go into politics one day,' said Brown.

'Whatever for? Do you think this will help?'

'It might.'

'But you can't tell anyone what you do.'

'I know. But I'd love to tell that woman in the office. And all those people who think it's just a game.'

'They don't care. You don't even like what you're doing. You don't even laugh about it.' I kicked off my boots. 'I could understand it if you enjoyed it. But you've done some of this stuff before. You don't enjoy it, and yet you're coming back for more!'

'I'm knackered,' said Brown, bending to untie his boots, 'and anyway look at me.' He was inspecting his sores. 'Nothing's healing. The food's crap. There's never any roughage in a military diet.'

At six-fifteen the following morning Birch conducted PT and for forty-five minutes we competed against the other sections in a series of relay races. Half-way through, Para tore a ligament in his knee and the medic excused him from the last twenty minutes. Since we were a man short, the OC joined our section. Cheating was therefore impossible.

'He's a fiend,' said the OC, referring to Birch.

Birch stood in the middle of the football pitch giving out concise instructions. He wore a long-sleeved, dark blue sweat-shirt, camouflaged trousers and boots. His warm breath condensed in the crisp air. He stood still and his gestures were controlled.

The OC was dressed like the rest of us and, in the dim light, he was barely distinguishable from the other recruits. He appeared to enjoy joining in and his enthusiasm was infectious.

'He's a fiend, lads,' the OC said again, grinning and bobbing about like a cork in the sea. 'His imagination is incredible. They cultivate it in 22. Watch out, lads. Here we go.'

'*Run!*'

We ran on all fours, this time sideways, monkey-like, from one end of the pitch to the other. At the far end we did thirty press-ups, before running back, the same way, and touching the next man. Next, we rolled forwards, head over heels, from one end of the pitch to the other as fast as we could. It was a sickening experience at any time of day, but twenty minutes after waking up it was monstrous.

'It's freefall training,' said the OC excitedly.

We yelled words of encouragement at our own men and abuse at the others. 'Come on, sir,' we shouted, delighting in the reversal of roles. 'Push it. Push it. You can do it, sir. Come on, drive it home . . . Well done, sir. Well done.' When we won, the OC was as happy as a schoolboy who scores the winning goal on home ground.

Fifteen minutes later the Sergeant-Major took parade.

'Brown, what's wrong with your helmet?' he said, stopping to examine the peculiar way it sat on his head.

'I don't know, sir.' Brown stood rigidly to attention.

'Something's wrong.' The Sergeant-Major twisted his head to look more carefully at the arrangement. There were only two or three straps on the helmets we wore, and the ways of joining them were extremely limited, yet Brown had contrived to produce a puzzle. And it was this enigmatic contortion of straps that seemed to fascinate the Sergeant-Major.

Genuinely perplexed, he said, 'Is the helmet too small for you, or is it your head?'

'I think it's my head, sir.'

The Sergeant-Major looked distressed, and said, 'There's not much we can do about that.' But then, after a pause, he grinned broadly and said, 'Legally.'

We spent the rest of the morning practising crossing obstacles. There was no secret to crossing a barbed-wire fence. If one had long legs, straddling it silently was easy. A noiseless crossing, however, if one was blessed with short legs, was virtually impossible. Any accidental twang would travel the full length of the wire, and a catch in the groin was guaranteed to induce a sound.

There was a secret to crossing a gate at speed. It came naturally to those taught the scissors method of high jumping at school. The technique was the same save that, on a gate, a hand could be used to gain extra height. Brown went to a smart school in London where such athleticism was neither taught nor encouraged. He failed at every attempt. I could imagine him trying to leap-frog a large box in the gymnasium and landing on his crotch every time.

To cross a drystone wall silently and at speed was the most difficult. The idea was to approach the wall confidently, step into it, and throw oneself, shoulder first, onto the ridge, so that for a fraction of a second one was lying on top of the wall, looking up into the sky. The theory was that momentum would preserve the roll, and one would land facing the correct way, on both feet on the other side. And no stone would be dislodged.

The demonstration was polished, but master this I could not. I could launch myself onto the wall but not without pain. We wore webbing and mine contained a mess tin, the rim of which dug straight into my kidneys. Once I remained on the wall, like a tortoise on its back, as I had insufficient momentum to carry me on, a target for a sniper. More often I came crashing down on the other side bringing a good bit of the wall with me. Repeated practice took successively deeper layers of skin off my hands as I landed clumsily in a pile of rubble.

Back at the barracks in the afternoon we stood, caked in mud, in the corner of the parade-ground waiting for Falstaff to hose us down.

One of the officers in 23 SAS looked at Brown and said, 'What's your name?'

'Brown, sir.'

'Brown,' he said, in his broad Geordie accent, 'I've been watching you. You're like an athletic spider.' And then, turning to the corporal who was with him, but still within earshot, said, 'How are we going to get rid of him? We can't have a man who looks like that in the regiment.'

The corporal smiled.

As the pair of them walked back across the parade-ground, the officer said, 'He always looks such a fucking misery.'

The next day, after PT and breakfast, the OC joined the Sergeant-Major for room inspection. We had worked frantically, and with astonishing cohesion, in the few minutes between PT and breakfast to sweep the floors, make our beds, empty the rubbish and remove all our clothes, stained white with salt, from the radiators. Sweaty socks went hard and brittle if, after having been worn for three or four days inside wet boots, they were left to bake on the radiators.

The Sergeant-Major toured our room from left to right. The OC knew everyone's name up to and including Brown's. Then he came to me. He stood at the end of my bed and looked into my eyes. 'I can't remember your name.'

'Ballinger, sir,' I replied, already standing to attention.

He nodded and moved on.

When they had finished inspecting both halves of the dormitory, Brown turned to me and said, 'The perfect grey man.'

'I can't believe it,' I said. 'We see him every week and he still doesn't know my name.'

'Why should he? You've never had to go and see him. He knows me because of my performance in the CFT. He knows Fowkes and Cordwell because they often used to come in first and second on Selection. He knows Para because he tried to wear his own boots.'

'Scott knows my name.'

'Yes, but that's not surprising. It's his job to know the men in his squadron. He knows all of us. The OC's not interested in names anyway. He couldn't learn them all. There'd be no point. Eighty per cent disappear in the first few weeks.'

Brown stared at me. 'You're lucky,' he said.

We spent the day shooting on the ranges. At dusk, we drove in four-tonners back to the training area, and practised patrolling through the elliptical depression. I naively expected a short stroll around the chestnut woods with one or two obstacles to cross. Not a bit of it. We walked east for four hours. Darkness fell. Nine sections of six men moved discreetly across the countryside, each accompanied by a corporal. Spike led us and remained silent.

Eventually we joined a tank track and after a mile or two, at a junction of three tracks, we were met by Falstaff for another lecture on night vision and night sounds. His props included a Chieftain tank, a Land Rover and a machine gun set to fire a few dozen rounds of blanks.

He radioed for the tank first and as it passed us we perched on the gravel track on our elbows and knees to feel the vibration. I could hear and feel this tank long before I could see it. When finally it did go past, about ten yards from my head, the shudder was intense. A revolving searchlight, with the power of one and a half million candles, served to highlight its sinister outline.

Next came the Land Rover. It stopped in the darkness one hundred yards away. Several men got out.

Falstaff pounced on Fowkes. 'You! What's your name?'

'Fowkes, sir.'

Falstaff paused, as if mentally recording his name, while the tank rumbled away in the distance. 'When I'm talking, you shut up and listen.

'How many men got out?'

'I don't know, sir.'

''Course you don't know. You weren't fucking watching. You were too busy talking.'

'Sorry, sir,' said Fowkes, looking down into the wet mud.

'How many men got out? How many were left inside? What were they doing? These are the sort of questions you should be asking yourself. How long are they staying, Fowkes? Where are they going?'

'I don't know, sir.'

'Think, Fowkes, think. This,' he said, pointing to his eye in the darkness, 'is a mark one eyeball. Use it.'

Seeing Fowkes struggling like a butterfly on a pin, Falstaff continued. 'Form a judgement, Fowkes. It depends on what they're wearing and what they're carrying. If they're carrying bergens, that tells you something, doesn't it, Fowkes?'

'Yes, sir.'

'What, Fowkes?'

'It means they're going for some time, sir.'

'Good. Very good. What would you deduce if one of them was carrying a spade, Fowkes?'

'I'd say they were going digging, sir.'

'Fucking hell! You see, Fowkes, you have got a brain. In this regiment you use it. Is that clear?'

'Yes, sir.'

'Good.' Falstaff turned to address the rest of us. 'These are questions you should be asking yourselves. You ask them over and over again. It's the mark one eyeball. You can't beat it. It's what this regiment is all about.'

One of the men who had left the Land Rover quickly vanished.

'Where is he?' Falstaff asked. But since no one was sure, no answers were volunteered.

Two minutes later Falstaff told him to stand up and be identified. He was a few feet in front of us.

Finally Falstaff fired the machine gun by remote control. The distinctive crack pierced the silence. 'Listen to this,' he said. 'You won't ever forget it.'

In the morning we returned, by four-tonners, to the training area and continued to practise patrolling with the eight other sections well into the evening. We moved in the cover of ditches and trenches, all the time carrying our bergens, webbing and weapons. Where we encountered obstacles, they had to be crossed using the techniques we had been shown. Lunch and dinner were forgotten. Under the cover of darkness we moved silently and stealthily, like predators through the night, hunters and ourselves hunted.

In the early hours of the morning Spike stopped the six of us on the edge of one of the tall but compact pine woods. Attacks from snipers, in the form of Falstaff and Birch, were expected. We were allowed to sleep, four at a time, while the other two kept watch. For the remainder of the night I was on watch with Para every two hours. We were bumped twice. The first intruder was spotted by Ham, through his night-sight, when he was on watch. He challenged the sniper who then fired on us. Ham retaliated with the machine gun and woke me up. I was four feet away. We guessed it to be Falstaff. The second intruder came some hours later and the man on watch sent a few rounds into the woods. I was too tired to get up. Para snored throughout.

At six-thirty Spike ordered us, bedraggled as we were, to stand-to. It was raining hard and our sleeping bags were soaked. We stared blankly through the woods. Hungry, worn, unshaven and exhausted, we lay motionless on the wet grass waiting for first light. Dark, oppressive storm clouds rumbled overhead, like tanks gathering in the dawn.

'OK,' said Spike, when the first trace of colour licked at the bottom of the clouds, 'let's move.'

We trudged back to the barracks, bleary-eyed and hungry.

Once there, we were given leisure to clean our weapons. Mine was wet, grassy and already rusting. A long wooden bench ran down the corridor, just outside the armoury. Above the bench a series of windows faced the parade-ground. On the opposite side of the corridor was the strong-room where we stored our weapons. Strips of oily rag and large plastic margarine containers, half filled with gun oil, littered the bench. There was not enough room for fifty-four men to stand at this work-table, and many sat outside on the kerbstone bordering the parade-ground.

I had just dismantled my weapon, with the parts neatly laid out on the bench, when Scott came up to me and began to strip a light support weapon, the new British machine gun.

'How are you finding Camp?' he asked.

'It's all new to me.'

'How did you find the CFT?' he went on, his eyes squinting in their deep sockets. His cheeks were still blotchy with yellow-black bruises.

'It was all right,' I said. 'Long Drag was a lot worse.'

Scott unclipped the side of his weapon and slid out the working parts.

'A lot of people got warnings after the CFT.'

'Did they?'

'How did you find Selection, though?' continued Scott, unusually keen to keep the conversation going.

'It was OK.'

'But what about the way we did things?'

The question caught me by surprise and, for a while, I said nothing, not knowing what he really meant.

'Go on, say what you think. It's important.' There was a pause. 'What did you think of me?'

'You seemed quite hard at times,' I said, cautiously.

'We have to be.' Scott sounded dutiful. 'We get so many cunts with big ideas turning up for these selection courses. It's the only way to sort them out. You'd be the same if you ran Selection. Did you think I was too hard, then?'

Astonished at the way the conversation was going, I said, 'I know some blokes thought you were a bit severe.'

Scott untied his pocket cleaning kit and started to scrape the carbon off the bolt with a small wire brush. 'I knew you'd get through,' he said, changing the subject. 'It was never in doubt.'

I reassembled the components of my weapon and slid the working parts backwards and forwards to work in the oil.

'Did you go to university, Ballinger?'

'Yes,' I said.

'Where?'

I hesitated and then said, 'Oxford.'

Scott smiled, and laid down his wire brush. 'I've got two A levels. Do you think I could get in there, I mean to a university? I'd like to.'

'Why not? What do you do now, anyway?'

'I work in the City,' he said. 'Fucking hate it.'

I clipped my weapon back together and tied up my cleaning kit.

'Get through TQ and you'll be onto Continuation,' said Scott. 'You won't see me much then. I've got to do another Selection course. It starts in a few months' time.'

'Another batch of recruits.'

'Cunts, Ballinger.'

Avery, Brown, Cordwell, Fowkes and I sat down to dinner together. Sampson and Para sat at another table. There were no lectures that evening and dinner was unusually relaxed.

'What were you talking to Scott about this afternoon?' Cordwell asked, slurping his soup.

'He was asking me about Selection. He seemed concerned about the way he did things. I think it's the first time he's taken it.'

'He's a bastard,' said Cordwell, 'I hope you told him that.' Cordwell laid his spoon in his soup and picked a slice of white bread up off the table. He rolled it up and stuffed it into his mouth.

'We won't see much more of him now,' I continued. 'After Camp he's going back to do another Selection course.'

'Thank God for that,' said Cordwell, chewing his bread. He pushed his bowl of soup, still half full, into the middle of the table and started to cut into his chicken.

'Interrogation in a few days,' said Fowkes, 'and then back home.'

'You seem anxious to be off,' I said.

'I am. I've got a business to run. We're struggling at the moment. I phoned my partner last night. He's been working until midnight every day this week.'

'I suppose he thinks he's doing all the work.'

'He is. It's not fair on him. I'm going to have to work fucking hard when I get back to make up for this.'

'I wonder if I'll have a job when I get back,' said Avery.

'You'll be all right,' said Brown.

'Para lost his,' said Avery.

'It's not worth it,' said Fowkes. Like Cordwell, he too had given up on his meal and was satisfying his hunger with bread and jam. 'Your job's got to come first. I tried to explain that to the OC after Long Drag.'

'You did what?' said Cordwell.

'I told him my business has to come first.'

'You fucking idiot. You heard him. He kept talking about hard decisions. "One hundred per cent, lads." '

'It's got to come first.'

'For Christ's sake don't try to reason with the OC,' said Cordwell, drawn in by Fowkes' persistence.

'You can drop out of life for a while,' said Brown, with a plate of boiled potatoes steaming in his face. 'It's the same with jobs. I don't think it does you any harm. You just go back and pick up where you left off. No one seems to mind, and after a few months they don't even remember.'

'My job has really suffered,' said Fowkes, determined to hold onto his line of thought. 'When I go into a client meeting on Monday morning I have to keep telling myself not to swear. My partner says I'm too aggressive, and I'm usually totally fucked.'

'But you chose to come here,' said Avery.

After dinner we watched a film entitled 'Resistance to Interrogation'.

As the concluding music died down and the credits flashed up on the screen, a stunned silence filled the room.

The OC jumped up to switch on the lights and Birch stood up wearing his beret.

Standing in front of the screen, Birch said, 'The aims are simple: to survive, to avoid processing, and to escape. But on the exercise you will do, the last two of these are not options.'

He went on, 'According to the Geneva Convention for Prisoners of War, you must state your name in full, your rank, your date of birth and your army number. Otherwise you have a vocabulary of seven words: "I cannot answer that question, sir," or, if it's a woman, "ma'am." You say nothing else.'

And then he smiled. 'Come on,' he said, aware of the silence in the room, 'who's got a penis like a baby's arm?' No one answered but the stillness was punctured by the shuffle of chairs. 'Come on. Someone must. It's to your advantage if you do. You know what happens when they get cold. Your bollocks'll go like walnuts. You might be questioned by a woman. She'll tease you. Say nothing. Display no emotion.'

Birch told us what we could and could not do during interrogation. 'You carry no bric-à-brac, no rings, nothing. You cut the labels from your underpants. You give them nothing. You go into Tactical Questioning sterile, absolutely fucking sterile.'

'What about tattoos, sir?' someone asked.

'A tattoo is a mine of information. A man with a tattoo is a walking encyclopedia. The Paras among you, for once, are disadvantaged. You're going to have a hard time. You'll be interrogated by experts, members of the Joint Services Interrogation Board. Don't kid yourselves. These people are professionals; it's their job, and they're fucking good at it. They're trained and they do it all the time. We use them in 22. They like nothing more than to make a bloke in the SAS talk. They're bastards.

'Your aim is to survive and give nothing away. You must enter that little black box in your mind.'

Back in the dormitory, as I was getting into bed, Avery came in. 'I've just been to see the OC,' he said. His short, wiry, brown hair and receding hair-line gave him a dishevelled, scholarly look. 'He said my performance to date had been below that required. And that my train ticket home was nine-tenths written.' Avery clenched his teeth. 'Fuck it.'

'Don't worry,' said Brown, sitting up in his bed. 'At least he hasn't got rid of you. It's probably just a warning.'

'I don't understand it,' said Avery. 'He didn't really say why.'

'Did you ask him?'

'Yes. He just said it was a combination of things, my general performance. I know we came last on the stretcher race, but fuck, it's got to be more than that.'

'Where did you come in the CFT?' I asked.

'Near the back. But so did a lot of other people who've not seen the OC.'

Para came storming into the dormitory with his sleeves rolled up. He slammed the door shut and kicked the front of Brown's locker. He smashed his fist into the cabinet beside his bed and dropped onto the chair, his knuckles white and his hands shaking.

'The fucking bastard.'

Cordwell crossed the room and Para looked up through his blond fringe, his eyes bloodshot and cruel.

'The fucking bastard.'

Cordwell held out a packet of cigarettes. Para took one, his tattooed frame taut and quivering.

'Looks like Para's been to see the OC as well,' said Avery.

'I should stay well clear,' said Brown. 'He's been in a military gaol six times for violence.'

Another man, trying to join 23 SAS, came bursting into the room.

'Fucking hell. This is not even my job . . . It's not my career . . . I've a wife and kids at home . . . I'm still wound up . . . I've done all this before . . . I've been in the army . . . Still he's managed to fucking upset me . . . Fuck it. I'm going to the naafi for a beer.'

'The OC's wound nearly everyone up,' said Cordwell.

The following evening Spike briefed us, as a section, for the final exercise.

'I suppose this is it,' I said, looking at Brown.

'TQ's very controlled. It'll all be over in four days.'

This was nonchalance I couldn't share. 'But how do you feel?'

'Awful. I'm already weak,' said Brown. 'And hungry.' Everything from a tea-bag to a loaded magazine lay on his bed. 'We'll probably lose all track of time from now on.' Brown lifted his webbing, heavy with three hundred blank rounds, onto his shoulders and jumped up and down. 'Do I rattle?'

The moon was one-quarter full and it shone through the small, square window, high up above my bed. The fluorescent lights in the dormitory flickered. Nearly every man sat on his bed going through his equipment time and time again. Very few spoke.

Para walked through the archway and into our room. 'Here you are,' he said, passing me the cumbersome and heavy snipe-sight, 'you're lead scout.'

Spike had given each one of us a different role in the patrol, and it was my job to lead the way for the first twelve hours.

'Thanks,' I said, taking it from him and inwardly cursing. I sat on my bed and, picking up my weapon, removed the smaller, standard optics and clipped on the bulky infra-red sight.

'All set, Para?' said Brown.

Para hovered about at the end of my bed. He looked tired and drawn and his streaky blond hair was thick with grease. Cam cream and mud had been wiped across his face. A camouflaged weapon hung from his bony hand and pointed towards the floor. His oily fingers disappeared, dripping like tar, around the dark green pistol grip. The combination of metal and bone dangled like an unusually long arm.

Para nodded.

'Rehearsals in one hour,' said Spike, coming into the dormitory and addressing the three of us. 'Tell the others.'

An hour and a half later, when we had finished our rehearsals, Spike looked at me across the starlit parade-ground and said, 'OK, Ballinger, lead off.'

We walked for twenty kilometres, through woods, bogs and swamps, and over ubiquitous barbed wire, stopping just before dawn.

'I want you to dig a latrine, Ballinger,' Spike said, pointing to a depression at the foot of a pine tree, 'before first light.'

I dropped my bergen and webbing. Brown knelt behind a tree, with a loaded weapon, and kept watch.

'Here,' said Heel, crawling under the low, skeletal branches, and passing me an entrenching tool.

I tried to swing the spade but there was no room. When I did strike into the pine needles, the implement barely scored the roots.

'I've got to get this off,' I said to Brown, pulling my smock, sodden with sweat, from my shoulders. I dropped it onto the ground and it steamed, like a panting fox, in the cold night air.

'OK,' whispered Spike, coming up to Brown and me much later. 'That's enough. We can't have the men falling in it.'

Spike called us together, and we crawled under the branches and along the furrows to where he sat.

'Listen,' he said, softly. 'Somewhere out there, there's a regular infantry regiment. Even now they're looking for you. This is the highlight of their fucking year. Every one of them wants to catch a bloke in the SAS; think what it means to them. If they catch you, and it gets rough, for fuck's sake don't antagonize them.'

'How long are you staying with us, staff?' Brown asked.

'Wait and see. Ballinger, Ham, you're on watch first. McNeil, Para, you go next, then you two. Swap round every hour.'

Ham and I lay squashed up in a ditch, scanning different arcs in the woods. The ground was dry but visibility was poor.

'How do you feel, Ham?'

'Sick. And hungry. You?'

'Terrible.'

Ham rested his chin on the butt of his weapon and his eyes began to close. He fought to keep them half open. The tops of the trees rustled in the breeze, but no wind and very little light reached us.

'What does your wife do, Ham?'

'She's pregnant. That's why we got married. We were going to get rid of it, but I'm glad we didn't now.'

'Big wedding?'

'No. I'm a Catholic. My wife's a Jew.' Ham smiled, and the cam cream stretched with his face. His eyes opened again and he changed his posture. 'I'd only slept with three women before. It was nothing serious. I met them at parties – one night stands. I miss my wife, though.'

We stopped talking and sleep and hunger surfaced again. It was harder to fight them alone and in silence. Later, McNeil and Para came, concealed and wriggling like mottled snakes along the ditch.

'See anything?' Para asked in an anxious whisper.

'No,' I said.

We changed over. The cycle continued, and went on and on. We fought in pairs, empty and dog tired, against the monotonous daylight hours.

'Come on,' said Spike. 'Let's move.' By now it was dark. We crawled out of the compressed darkness of the woods, and into the open night. We walked on across the moors, always staying in the murky ground, searching and scanning for our captors, who, we knew for certain, would get us eventually. Birch would see to that: it was part of the exercise. Icy rain drove horizontally across the burnt heather, and we slunk, soaked, behind a drystone wall. Brown crouched down beside me and shook convulsively with cold.

'All right?' I asked.

He turned his head. Rain ran off the oily camouflage on his face, and his wet lips quivered with the chatter of his teeth. His eyelids drew together, like curtains, shutting out the whites of his eyes, and he nodded.

Hours, horrible grey, tumbling hours, slipped by.

We moved, eventually, and dropped down into a shallow ditch. Reeds grew for hundreds of yards across the marshy ground, and sighed in the wind, swamping the squelch of our boots. We moved from cover to cover, roving, homeless men with nowhere to go. Spike led us through the marsh to more dead ground and we followed him in silence. We crawled with our bergens on our backs, like snails, along a stony stream into more woods. The stars and the slender moon disappeared and, like rodents, we slipped back into the darkness.

One hour on, two hours off: the watch roster continued. The pairs changed. Para and I started the sequence. Para's eyes were blank, but forced wide, like a cat's.

'You look fucking terrible,' he said to me. 'Your eyes are like piss-holes in the snow.'

Hunger, silence and the droning monotony of it all were sapping us. The ligament that I tore on Long Drag failed to heal, and every bend, every twist, made my eyes water.

Para cursed. 'It can't be much fucking more.'

I lay blindfolded, face down on the back of a four-tonner. Steel rivets pushed hard against my forehead. Men lay, stacked like pipes, on top of me.

Suddenly the four-tonner stopped moving and the engine was switched off. Trees rustled in the cold wind, and I shivered. My shirt, heavy with perspiration, chilled my back and a bead of cold sweat slipped across my spine. I could feel the other men, wet and shaking, their combat clothes clinging to my clammy skin. A damp smock, and the dead weight of the man inside it, lay against my face.

Somewhere, a door opened and the hinges creaked. But then it slammed shut, and I jolted with the cold. Men came splashing through the mud, towards the back of the truck. My heart beat faster. They stood near the tail-gate, talking to one another in whispers. I strained to hear above my bounding pulse. The man on top of me was pulled away. There was a stifled grunt, a slip, and a kick.

Two men seized me by the arms and lifted me up. My legs followed, as they took the weight. Another man got kicked in the process. I was thrown out of the truck and fell to the muddy track below. The trees rustled again and suddenly the squelching stopped. Nobody moved. Water seeped through my clothes. Instinctively, I lifted my head out of the puddle, pushing against the sediment with my hands, and arching my back up out of the clay. When I pulled my hands from the sludge, it sucked noisily at my fingers. I knelt, shaking, with rainwater running down my face. It was quiet save for the trees. I tried to wipe my hands on my thighs, but when I moved two men grabbed me.

I was put in a room, I think. At least the wind stopped for a moment. I had to strip and remove the plasters covering my sores. I stood spread-eagled and at a painful angle against a wall. My hands were forced up against rough, damp stones above my head. My legs were kicked apart. But I could still hear the grunts and splashes, the swearing and shoving, as men were moved, like lethargic cattle, one at a time, from a truck to a barn.

A door was bolted. The clunk echoed and the wind was shut out. All movement seemed to stop and it went horribly quiet. My bare feet ached on the cold concrete floor. I could feel my calf muscles tightening, and the pain rising. My eyes were tightly closed beneath the blindfold, and yet pinpricks of light danced in front of me, stabbing at my vision.

I was sure there was a man to the left of me, not far away. I thought I could hear him breathing, but it was difficult above my own gasps. I tried to communicate with him by moving my hands, imperceptibly slowly, across the wall. I wanted to touch him, to know for certain that I was not alone. And yet I felt sure we were being watched. But by how many men? Surely, they could not watch all of us, all of the time?

I stretched out my fingers across the stones, and then moved up my palms to close the extension. I moved slowly and carefully, like a caterpillar in full view of a hungry thrush. I kept trying, until I could move my hands no further, until there was no more slack in my arms. I curled my toes and, for a moment, felt better: there was less skin on the icy floor. I tried to shift my weight onto the balls of my feet, to release my heels. I swivelled slowly. But then somebody yanked my arms back above my head, and it was worse, much worse: my fingers tingled, my shoulders stretched. The floor was freezing. I gulped in a mouthful of wintry air and exhaled erratically. I could hear footsteps. They got closer. And closer.

'It was during the war,' Hassan said. 'The Pakistan Army wanted to touch my mother. My brother, my crazy brother, did not want this. He shouted at the soldiers, but they laughed at him. He lashed out, at the face of the Pakistani, with a knife. He was a foolish man, sir. The soldier shot him. Then they shot my father.'

'Were you there?'

'No, sir. My uncle was, but he escaped. He ran away. When I went home my mother and sister had been stabbed. It was a very bad time for me, sir. My uncle told me what happened.' Tears filled his eyes.

The fields were lush and lined with dead animals. The carcasses were putrefying and the smell of rotting flesh lingered in the sticky heat.

'I think of suicide sometimes, sir.'

'But you have a baby girl now.'

'Yes. When I think of Jolie I want to live. I want her to go to school.'

'She is nearly two now, isn't she?'

'Yes, sir. Jolie's mother is growing up too. She is no longer a child. She is sixteen now.'

'You don't still hit her, do you?'

'Sometimes, but not in the face now, or on the chest.'

I was forced to bend my knees. One man pushed my shoulders down, another crossed my legs, stretching the torn ligament. I sat naked, on the concrete with my hands on top of my head. There was no freedom of movement. My hands were locked together and the weight of my arms pulled down on my joints. I could move my fingers and toes, but not my frame. I was rigid and stiff with cold. I squirmed on the floor, shuffling to preserve my balance, letting my head fall and my hands slip behind my neck. The change, however slight, was pleasurable. I felt dizzy. Faintness came in waves.

Later, two men lifted me to my feet again, but my legs would not straighten. The elasticity had gone. I was made to stand. Blood rushed to my feet and down my arms; it was almost comfortable. But then I was pushed back against the wall. The shuffle of boots on concrete began again. It sounded like two men. They stopped, not far away. Grunts, slaps and the gasps of a surprised man filled the room. They took him somewhere. There was stamping and a struggle. A bolt slid. A door was blown back on its hinges and crashed against a stone wall. It swung back and forth in the gale. I could hear the trees once again: the wind whistled through the branches. There were splashes and thuds outside, and then nothing above the howl of the wind.

I breathed, shaking as I inhaled, and felt my ribs push against my skin. I felt light-headed and cold, seriously cold. My fingers splayed across the uneven stones, feeling for holes, cracks, something to concentrate on. Touch. A sensation. But then a fist slammed into my kidneys: my arms had slipped too far down the wall. My fingers had moved, curiously, like a cat, searching for a new hole, something else: a bigger picture. I struggled to hold up my arms, but the circulation had slowed and they became almost too heavy.

The aching went on, hour after hour: pain always returning. At some stage I was pulled away from the wall, out of the building and into the mud. Inside and out – I knew that much. More pushing, frogmarching, manhandling . . .

'How did your son die?'

Hassan moved in his chair uncomfortably. 'Something wrong with his mother.'

'Was she ill?'

'Yes, yes she was. She killed him. She stabbed him, sir, with a chicken bone. He was seven months old. No money, sir,' Hassan said, reading my thoughts. 'No money, no food.'

'What did you do?'

'I beat her, sir. She was fourteen. She is learning now: we are growing closer together.'

*

I was left standing. A door had been closed behind me. Stillness. My arms hung heavy by my sides and I could feel my fingers tingling as the blood returned. Someone removed the blindfold. After three days without sleep my eyes were sore and unfocused, and I could hardly see. Slowly, I made out a man dressed in black with a crew cut who looked at me without blinking. He sat behind a dirty desk, on which he had laid out my possessions: boots, laces, soggy clothes, a crumpled, blood-stained plaster, a compass, an oily handkerchief. A pathetic assembly, but enough to keep me warm. Another member of the Joint Services Interrogation Board moved nervously behind him.

I stood under a lone light bulb and alongside an empty chair. Crew Cut pointed to it. Nobody spoke. I sat down, naked, and stretched out my legs, allowing my arms to hang limply over the side of the wooden seat. There was no position I had to maintain, no posture I had to hold.

'Stand up!' he shouted. '*Stand up, I said.*'

I stood up slowly but allowed myself to shiver. My teeth chattered and the door rattled on its hinges.

He picked up my blue Biro from the table and used it to point at my genitals, pulled tight after hours of cold. 'Find it exciting, do you?' he said. The man behind him looked at me and laughed.

'I asked you a question,' Crew Cut continued.

'I cannot answer that question, sir.'

'That's not a question, fuckhead. This is a question, "Find it exciting, do you?" and the answer is, "Yes, sir, I'm going to come all over my foot." Got it?'

Crew Cut looked at me and then at the other man. Still facing him, he said, 'He's not got a foreskin. It's a pity.' And then turning to me, he smiled. 'Some men try to hide things under there. Did you know that?

'What's your name?'

'Adam Ballinger.'

'Fucking hell, progress. Now we're getting somewhere.' The man's skin looked unnaturally pale, against the black of his leather jacket.

The questions and the commands went on and on. The commands were humiliating, and the questions rolling, manipulative and twisting. But then, quite suddenly, having ascertained my name, number and date of birth, Crew Cut decided he'd had enough. The blindfold was put on again.

All too soon I was back against the wall, arms and legs apart. I tried to measure time by counting the intervals between the waves of dizziness, but they were not the same length. Time was no longer in my frame of reference. I could measure amplitude, the extent of pain, but that was all.

My bowels grumbled even though I had eaten nothing for days. And I needed a piss. 'Just go,' Birch had said. 'Just crap on the floor, where you are.' I tried to hold it, telling myself that it was just my stomach melting, that it was only acid; that my dignity was worth more than that. But I dribbled onto the floor.

'You're an intelligent man,' she said, looking at me through her smeared glasses. 'Why are you here?'

'I cannot answer that question, ma'am.'

'Oh, no. I don't expect you to. I'm not trying to catch you out. You're far too clever for that. Just listen.'

She walked about the large room that looked like a white-washed stable and I could smell the perfume on her. I sat on the only chair in the middle, under a small spotlight. The corners of the room were in darkness. One hand stroked her plump chin and the other held the bent elbow.

'You people interest me,' she said. 'What regiment are you in?'

'I—'

'It's all right. I know. But I don't understand you. You sound like an intelligent man. I expect you went to university, didn't you? . . . No. Don't answer. I told you not to. I'm just thinking aloud.

'Why should an intelligent man, who, let us say, has been to a good university, put himself through this? Have you any idea what time it is?'

'I cannot—'

'Ssh. I'm talking. You could be doing anything you liked now.

You could be at home reading a book. I expect you'd like that, a thoughtful man like you. You could be with your girlfriend. Just think. What a thought. I wonder if she knows you're here now and with me, like this. I'm sure she wouldn't like it.' My interrogator giggled. 'Would she?'

'I cannot answer that question, ma'am.'

'You could be doing anything, anything you liked, but you choose to do this. You've got to admit, it's surprising, isn't it?'

'I cannot—'

'You stupid *wretch*. You chose to go hungry. You chose not to sleep. Look at you, cuts, scabs, you're even bleeding. You disgusting little creature.

'What's your name?'

'Adam Ballinger.'

'Adam Ballinger, do you know what you are?'

'I cannot answer that question, ma'am.'

'You don't have to. I'll tell you what you are: you're a fucking idiot. I try to reason with you, and you respond like a mindless man. I gave you the credit of having a brain, but I was mistaken, wasn't I?'

The cycle of probing, ensnaring questions went on, before, once again, I was taken away. Later, I was marched into another room, and stood in silence for a few minutes. I could hear the birds and the familiar rustle of leaves blowing in the wind. It was dawn, the last dawn.

The blindfold was removed and I was debriefed by an unfamiliar member of the Interrogation Board, also in a black leather jacket.

'You did all right,' he said. 'You did not antagonize your interrogators, you were polite and you gave nothing away. I have graded your performance as "fine".' But he did not say what 'fine' meant.

At the end of the debrief, the medical officer, who was sitting quietly in the corner, threw me a plastic bin liner containing my clothes. I put them on and laced my boots using random eyelets. Still clutching the black plastic bag I walked, like a tramp, out into the daylight, away from the compound and the copse of trees, towards the minibus. Two other recruits sat together in the back of the bus shivering furiously. I offered one my wet jumper and he took it, but it did little to warm him up.

We were just about to drive back to the sprawling barracks when the OC came running through the trees and up to the minibus. Banging on the window and looking at me, he said, 'Get out here, Wilkins. *Move!*'

I swung back the door and jumped out onto the grass verge.

'What the fuck do you think this is? You might have scored a "fine", but fucking hell, no man on this course has an unfair advantage. No man who has worked for the Interrogation Board goes into TQ without telling me. I shall see you, Wilkins,' he said, hopping about on the grass and shaking with fury, 'back at the barracks.'

'But, sir,' I said, when he had finished, 'I'm not Wilkins.'

The OC looked shocked. 'Who are you then?' he spluttered.

'Ballinger, sir.'

'You're not Wilkins?'

'No, sir.'

'Shit. I've been wasting my breath on the wrong man?'

'Wilkins is in Three Squadron, sir.'

The OC started laughing. 'You're in such a state you all look the fucking same.' But then he remembered Wilkins. 'Well, I've just discovered that that cunt used to work for those people. Where is he now?'

'I don't know, sir. I've only just come out myself.'

'OK. Get back in there,' he said, pulling at the door of the minibus, 'and get yourself cleaned up at the barracks. And make sure none of the other regiments there see you looking like that. And that goes for all of you,' he said peering into the bus.

We were driven back to the barracks in threes and fours as men were released. Once there, we ate and washed for the first time in several days.

*

On Sunday morning we filed into the lecture theatre for the OC's debrief and the closure of Camp. The OC stood up on the small platform at the front and addressed us all. We were no longer required to remain in our sections and I sat with Avery and Brown.

'I'm disappointed, lads,' he began. 'More than half of you gave something away during TQ. That's more than twenty-seven men. It's a fucking disgrace. It's a weakness, lads. I've got your debrief papers here: it's all recorded.

'Some of you said just a "yes" or a "no". It might not sound much, but fucking hell, it's enough. It's like the PSI said, these people are experts. You haven't got to be too bright, lads, to take a yes and a no on a tape-recorder and mix them with different questions. Think about it. It's the grey matter,' he said, pointing to the side of his head. 'That's what this regiment's all about.

'Some of you were carrying notebooks with writing in. One of you even had a set of grid references written down. And that's fucking serious, lads. That man goes no further. One of you had a camera. Jesus, think, just think. What happened to the holiday snaps: mum, dad, sister and the rest? I've said it before, lads, and I'll say it again: this is not the fucking Girl Guides.

'Right, lads, we don't usually do this,' the OC looked downcast. 'If a man fails on this course I interview him on his own, but this time, there's too many of you. And I want to go home today. So I'm going to read out a list of everyone who, as far as I'm concerned, has passed this Camp. In other words, if your name appears on this list you go on to Continuation.'

We sat in silence. One side of the lecture theatre faced the football pitch, and it was there that Birch had led us so often for PT. On the other side, the windows faced the parade-ground, where we had formed up, in our sections, almost every morning for inspection. Coaches, four-tonners and Land Rovers, already loaded with our belongings, were parked on the square. In a few minutes men trying to join 21 and 23 SAS, who had come together for Camp, would, if they passed, return to their own squadrons for further tests.

'Listen in, lads,' the OC began. 'I'll call out your names alphabetically.'

The room went very quiet and we listened for the names we knew.

'Avery.'

Avery heaved a sigh of relief: he had passed despite the OC's warning.

'Ballinger, Brown—'

Brown smiled. The comments from the officer in 23 SAS with the Geordie accent had come to nothing.

'—Cordwell . . . Fowkes . . . Ham, Heel . . . McNeil . . . Sampson . . .'

But when he got to Sampson we ceased to listen. It was Avery who spoke first. He leant across to me and whispered, 'Para's not there.'

THE RITZ

The very sensitive need a woman to be easy of
access if crystallization is to be encouraged.

                                        Stendhal

A few days later we returned to the One Squadron barracks for the
first drill night of Continuation.

'What happened to Para, then?' I asked, as I took off my suit.

'I expect he said something during interrogation,' said Brown.

'No he didn't.' Cordwell slipped his braces off his barrel chest.
'I went out for a drink with him when we got back, and he said he
didn't say anything.'

'He must have done,' said Brown.

But just then Scott walked past the changing room and, seeing
us, stepped inside. The discoloration had gone from his face, but
his skin was still unnaturally dark. He looked around the room and,
noticing the number of empty pegs, said, 'You've got a lot more
room now. Back in April you couldn't move in here.'

Cordwell spoke first, and rather abruptly. 'Why did you get rid
of Para, staff?'

Scott scanned the room, checking that we were only six. 'He had
the wrong mental attitude.'

Avery, Brown, Cordwell, Fowkes, Sampson and I fell in on the
parade-ground and awaited the OC. We stood in two rows of
three. The lime trees on the edge of the square had shed their leaves,

stripping the barracks of almost all colour. Even the sky was a tarmac grey. All that remained was a matt-green Land Rover, parked outside the storeroom, with a red cross painted on the side.

The OC looked out of his office window and, spotting us, came outside in his sharply creased uniform and weathered beret. 'OK, lads,' he said eagerly, 'don't worry about parade. Follow me.'

He led us into the familiar classroom and we sat down. The desks still rocked and the chairs had not changed, but there was plenty of space. All the unused furniture lay stacked at the far end of the room. Birch followed us in, closed the door, and remained standing in front of the light switch.

The OC nodded at him and laid down his notes on the lectern. 'Right, lads: Continuation, the third and final phase of Selection. Listen carefully, there's a lot to take in.' And then, noticing us pick up our pens, he said, 'Don't take notes, lads. Just listen.

'Continuation is a bit different. The purpose from now on is to train you for your sabre squadrons. You'll be learning some of the basic SAS skills. But don't get me wrong, you can still fail and one or two always do. The emphasis now is on instruction. There will still be tests, but you've done Long Drag and TQ, so you've proved something. It's not much, but it's something. I look at you now, lads, as the sort of blokes I might, and only might, want in this regiment. But you've got to prove yourselves. It's not the grey man principle now: you've got to show me that you can become fucking good soldiers.'

The OC turned over his first sheet of paper and said, 'Any questions so far?'

No one spoke.

'Right, the format. The format will be the same as during Selection. Drill nights will be once a week, and our exercises will take place on alternate weekends. Same rules: no absentees. The first weekend exercise is in ten days' time, and that's the river crossing test. You've got to pass it.'

At this the OC suddenly looked serious. 'River crossing is a fucking dodgy business, lads. This regiment has lost more men through casualties in the water than by any other means. Men have died on these exercises. When your PSI briefs you, listen very carefully.' He looked across at Birch before resuming.

'You'll join up with the other four squadrons in 21 for the weekends, just as you did for Selection. And on some of them I shall be splitting you into patrols. Team work, lads, that's what it's all about. In this regiment you've got to be able to work on your own, and in patrols.

'Drill nights will be devoted to lessons. There's a lot to get through in the next four to five months: chemical warfare, first aid, patrolling, SAS tactics, and more. I'm afraid you're going to be spending a good bit of your time in this classroom. At the end of the course you will have written exams in all of these, so take copious notes.

'Right, this brings me to my next point, and that's fitness.' The OC turned another page. 'From now on, there'll be no Corporal Scott helping you. You've got to train alone. Run together if you prefer. But I warn you, in this regiment we demand the highest possible standards. There're a lot of bergen runs on Continuation and they'll soon sort out who's not fit enough. Just cast your minds back to the CFT, lads. Think about it. You've got ten days to sharpen your fitness.'

The OC stopped talking and stood back. His beret sat perfectly on his head, and the crisp creases in his shirt were accentuated in the fluorescent light of the lectern. Viewed on his own the OC was not noticeably small, but when taken alongside Birch he looked just as a sparrow would appear in the shadow of a falcon.

'From now on,' he continued, 'I shall be taking a back seat. I shall be watching you, but your PSI will be organizing most of the weekends and taking your lessons.

'You're privileged, lads, all the other squadrons in this regiment are taught by their own corporals. They see us only at weekends. You've got the best. That's the advantage of having your squadron location at the HQ. You've got no excuses. I don't want to see any failures from now on.'

When he had finished he jumped down from the platform and Birch stepped up to take his place. If anything, the extra fifteen inches served to increase his presence. Birch took off his beret, laid it on the lectern and switched off the fluorescent light. He had no notes.

'I remember you,' said Birch, looking straight at Cordwell. 'You're the one who came out of TQ grinning like a Cheshire cat.

'And you. You're Avery aren't you?'

'Yes, sir.'

'Last in the log race?'

'I'm afraid so, sir.'

'Fowkes, isn't it?' he said, looking at Fowkes and his creased shirt. 'Lucky there was no inspection tonight, weren't we?'

'Yes, sir.'

Birch smiled. Unlike the OC he appeared to wear what he liked and his preference seemed to be for camouflaged T-shirts that matched his mottled trousers.

'What's your name?'

'Sampson, sir.'

'And yours?'

'Ballinger, sir.'

'Brown, sir.'

'We've got the rest of this evening and next week before your first weekend. This week I'm going to start the chemical warfare course, which usually lasts about ten weeks, but next week I want to spend half the evening on river crossings.'

Birch chattered away for an hour and we sat spellbound, listening to his jokes and anecdotes, before realizing that he had just delivered a lecture on the different types of chemical agents and we had failed to take any notes.

'It's all right,' said Birch, noticing our plight at the end of his lecture. 'It's all on the hand-outs.' And he proceeded to give out summaries, in tabulated form, of everything he had said.

At the end of the evening, we collected locker keys and NBC suits from the Storeman and were directed to a row of grey steel cupboards.

'Who went to work on Monday, then?' said Cordwell, trying to get his key to work.

'I didn't,' I said. 'I took the day off.'

'I went to work,' he said, 'and it was a fucking wash-out. I've been fucked all week. Mind you, I never knew I could go for four days with no sleep at all. Even at Cambridge I didn't do that.'

'What did you do with your day off?' Brown asked, looking at me.

'I took my girlfriend to the Ritz.'

'You did what?' said Cordwell.

'I took her out for tea and the first thing she said was, "Did you enjoy your holiday?"'

Brown burst out laughing. It was the first time we had seen him really laugh and it was more of a sudden, short-lived titter than an unrestrained roar.

'What did you say?' Brown asked, when he had finished giggling.

'I hope you told her,' said Cordwell, 'it was fucking boring and the food was crap.'

'I kept falling asleep and she said, "You look tired." When I told her I had hardly slept last week, she said, "How stupid. I hope you're not expecting any sympathy."'

'Well, my girlfriend chucked me on Sunday night,' said Cordwell. 'I phoned her up when we got back and that was the first mistake. She came round late and as soon as we got into bed, I crashed out. She went berserk.'

'They don't understand,' said Fowkes. Fowkes was busy undressing. He removed each item and threw it into the bottom of his locker. When he was down to his underpants he slung his boots on top of the pile and quickly slammed the door shut, to prevent the contents from pouring out onto the floor. 'I've never met a woman who likes the army,' he said, turning the key. 'It's best not to tell them. You have to let them know when you can see them and when you can't. If they don't like it, it's too bad. There's plenty of them about.'

'I got rid of my girlfriend on Monday,' said Sampson. 'It was too much hassle. I can't do this and worry about a girlfriend. I told her I was quite happy if she just wanted sex, but she wanted all the bloody rest as well. Dinner with her mother and all that.'

Sampson sat alongside Avery. They were both heavy, pale-skinned men, but Avery was a lot less muscular.

'It looks like you're the only one with a girlfriend, then,' said Brown.

'She'll give you up soon enough,' said Cordwell.

We put our civilian clothes back on and, just as we were leaving the locker room, Fowkes clapped Avery on the shoulder. 'Don't forget, self-defence classes on Thursday. Come to my place at seven.'

We gathered again a week later for the second drill night. Brown and I were the first to arrive.

I lifted my boots from the locker and sat down on the wooden slats to polish them. 'It seems ridiculous at times,' I said. 'Two thirty-minute interviews and I could probably change my job, and earn a lot more money than I get where I am. I did the five-mile run fifteen months ago, and there's still another four to five months to go.'

'Scott managed it,' said Brown, picking up his boots. 'Can I borrow your polish?'

'It's the thought of Scott that keeps me going. It proves it's actually possible.'

'What does your girlfriend do?' asked Brown, changing the subject.

'She's a GP.'

'Will you marry her?'

I hesitated. 'Yes. We're engaged. I'm getting married at the end of the course.'

Brown smiled. 'Does the OC know?'

'No. I'm not telling him either, especially after what he said on the way back from Long Drag. You're the only one who knows.'

'What does your future wife think about this?'

'I haven't told her.'

'But surely she knows?'

'Why? I suppose I'll have to tell her one day.'

Fowkes came in, accidentally kicked the tin of polish across the floor, and opened his locker. A pair of boots fell out into his arms and he winced.

'Are you all right?' I asked.

'Not too bad. Played rugby on Saturday and broke three ribs. I had terrible stabbing pains for the rest of the game.'

'You didn't stop?'

''Course not. We were winning.'

'What about this weekend coming?'

'Oh, they'll be better by then.'

Brown retrieved the tin of polish. 'Have you seen a doctor? A broken rib can puncture your lungs.'

'Too late now. We're off on Friday. I'm sure they'll be better by then, anyway.'

That evening, Birch continued to lecture on chemical warfare and the different types of biological agents. In the second half, he ran through the different methods of crossing rivers, all of which involved swimming. The skill, so Birch said, lay in floating the bergens and in choosing the optimum crossing point. When he had finished we returned to the locker room.

'Who's coming for a run?' Sampson asked.

'I will,' I replied.

'I'm coming,' said Cordwell.

'Two minutes,' said Fowkes.

Avery and Brown declined.

The four of us set off towards the running track. It was a cold, wet, wintry evening, and the track was mostly obscured by piles and drifts of fallen leaves.

'Let's go around London,' said Cordwell.

Characteristically, he set a quick, unrelenting pace that did not ease up for the weak. I was not feeling strong. Soon, too soon, Cordwell was running effortlessly faster. Sampson and I leant into the head wind, but Cordwell quickly ran off into the distance. We ran on, pushing against the wind as we might push against the sea when trying to run through it. Drizzling rain soaked our T-shirts. Sampson and I continued to squeeze out miles in less than six minutes, but it hurt me terribly. We ran, steaming in the cold rain, for about forty minutes until we caught sight of the barracks again. The wind dropped, I filled my lungs with air and tried desperately to stay with Sampson as he led us home. Cordwell, fully recovered, watched us come in.

I looked at Sampson: thirteen and a half stone of bone and muscle stood sweating before me.

'I'm shattered,' I said, struggling to stand upright.

Cordwell smiled and showed no signs of being the slightest bit tired. He looked as if he was ready to go out again.

Sampson said, 'Cordwell used to run for Cambridge.'

'Why didn't you tell me?' I panted.

'Didn't want to spoil the surprise.'

SWIMMING

Service life in this way teaches man to live largely on little.

T. E. *Lawrence*

Avery sat in front of me in the locker room, grinning as he often did with an air of intellectual satisfaction. He had at last managed to purchase a copy of *Eastern Approaches*, at my recommendation, from a second-hand bookshop in South Devon. While at Oxford he had toyed with the idea of entering politics, but, unlike Brown, had now given up on the idea.

'Read "Feet on the Gravel",' I said, as he unwrapped the book.

'Eight forty-eight hour exercises to go,' I said, but Avery paid no attention.

'Good grief, what a way to enter Parliament.'

We were going to join up with the other seven recruits for the first weekend of Continuation. Of these, four men were trying for Two Squadron, two were trying for Three Squadron, and one man was going for Four Squadron. We had lost Para as a consequence of Camp; Two Squadron had lost one man and Three Squadron, two.

We left the barracks on a Friday evening and drove to the training area we had used for the first weekend of Selection. We did not, however, return to the aircraft hangar. We drove instead to a bunker numbered XX and arrived shortly after midnight.

The bunker was no more than a derelict barn. We stepped inside and immediately splashed into a deep puddle; water was pouring in through a hole in the roof. Wet dung had been shovelled into piles in the corners, and the floor hastily swept. A rusty gas cooker stood in one corner behind a flimsy cardboard partition. A soggy sandpit for modelling the surrounding countryside had been left, with one or two sticks and pieces of string, in the middle of the floor. Some old airline seats had been propped up against the back wall and mould was growing on the damp upholstery. Two dim light bulbs hung from the corrugated iron roof, and they swung in the draught. Outside, a rusty oil drum stood collecting the rainwater. A mobile generator rattled away and supplied the electricity. There was no latrine and the back of the bunker was rank with human waste. A large grassy embankment surrounded the building so that it was scarcely visible from the outside or above. Stripped of all comforts save a roof, this was an eerie place. Anything, I thought, could happen here, and no one would ever know.

The sound of the generator and the dangling light bulbs reminded me of the room in which I had been interrogated two weeks before. A few dozen mattresses, going green with mildew, were stacked near the sandpit. We dropped our bergens against one of the walls and Avery and I both took one of the mattresses. We looked at each other simultaneously and smiled.

'You pansy,' he said.

We dragged our rotting mattresses onto a dry bit of the concrete and tried to sleep, but it was not easy. At four-thirty in the morning I woke Avery. It was our turn to keep watch. We stood outside by the generator, watching the rain fall.

'How are the self-defence classes going?' I asked, trying to break the monotony.

'They're good, but I'm still bloody stiff. The instructor's so fast, you can't see him move. Fowkes thinks he's Egyptian but I'm convinced he's Japanese. He wanted to do a demonstration and, like a fool, I volunteered. He had me all over the fucking floor.'

Avery's cap-comforter hid most of his wiry brown hair, but a few wet strands draggled down onto his forehead. Raindrops, clinging to the woollen headgear, glistened in the moonlight.

'Do you have any other interests?'

He raised the sights on his weapon and, turning the switch on the side to night vision, peered through them into the darkness. 'War films,' he said, grinning, and lowering the weapon.

At five-fifteen we began the first of many bergen runs. This one was a four-mile run across country with a thirty-pound load and a weapon. Birch led the way and kept us going at a fraction under ten miles per hour. We scarcely slowed for the hills except one, which was very long and steep, and in this case he dropped the pace to a jog. As we approached the bunker at the end of the circuit I began to wind down, but Birch ran straight past. I feared another four-mile lap but after a mile we about-turned and ran back to the bunker. When we arrived five men were already there. They had given up after the first circuit. Brown was one of them. When the OC, who accompanied us, saw them he was livid.

'*You!*' The OC pointed his bony finger at Brown. 'You, Brown, are not fit enough for this regiment. You have got some serious work to do. Understand?'

'Yes, sir,' said Brown, standing in the cold drizzle and looking dejected.

It was still dark. Rainwater and sweat ran down our faces. Our trousers were sodden with mud and my parade boots were caked with clay like a pair of farmer's wellingtons.

'You might think you have passed Selection, lads, but it's not over yet,' the OC continued. 'Not by a fucking long way.'

We squelched into the bunker and sat down on our filthy mattresses. I opened my cardboard box of rations and tried to make a reasonable breakfast.

The OC then divided us across squadrons into patrols of four and five. Each patrol was to be commanded by a member of the regiment, either a lance corporal or a corporal, and it was his job to watch us. He needed to be sure he could work with us and we could work with him. His word was final and it was up to him whether or not he reported any misdemeanours on our part either to Birch or to the OC. I was separated from the surviving members of my own squadron and put in a patrol with four other recruits. Fatty, Will and Jim came from Two Squadron and Gordon came from Three Squadron.

Fatty was tall, curly-haired and, compared to the rest of us, plump. He had small beady eyes, was an accomplished water-colourist and, like Falstaff, smoked an S-shaped pipe. He had read Music at university. After graduating he moved to France where he had worked for three or four years as an opera singer with a French touring company. He left to try to join 21 SAS.

Will and Jim were both small. Will had short, mousy hair and, as a civilian, sold portable computers. He was, apparently, the richest man in Two Squadron. Jim, like Scott, worked in the City of London. He had not been to university. It was his aim, if he passed the course, to try to join the regular SAS, although he seldom admitted this. During Selection Will and Jim had become good friends and, on the weekends between our exercises, they frequently went to France to look at First World War graves. Gordon was taller than the rest of us and noticeably more quiet than the men in Two Squadron. He was polite, softly spoken, married and father of a two-year-old girl.

Spike was to be our patrol commander (PC). Spike was a corporal in Three Squadron and he knew Gordon well. He knew me from Camp.

Thirteen of us left the bunker in darkness and patrolled across the training area towards some scrub land. Spike led the way and, after about an hour, we prepared an ambush in dead ground overlooking a deserted Land Rover track.

We guessed that the men who would walk into the ambush would be Birch and the OC but we had not been told when. We were given blank rounds, thunderflashes and smoke grenades. 'You may have to lie in an ambush for several days, or even weeks,' Birch had told us that afternoon. 'I was in a patrol that waited for three weeks once. And if they're not dead after contact,' he had continued, 'and you don't need them alive, put a few more rounds in. Aim for the head. Don't fuck about: you haven't got time.'

We lay waiting in the damp grass for several hours, our bodies chilling rapidly against our cold, wet clothes. I shivered, felt tired and struggled to keep my eyes open. I was just about to doze off when a burst of automatic fire and a grenade brought me to my senses. The grenade shook the ground and the vibration thumped my ribs. Spike lit two thunderflashes and we sent bursts of automatic fire into the ambush. Seconds later we were a gang of aggressive men. Pairs left the protection of the scrub and quickly searched Birch and the OC. They were half stripped and valuables taken. Like a mob of armed thieves protected by darkness, we left the scene of our crime rapidly. We left nothing save two men on their backs, dead still.

Two hours later I was in my sleeping bag. We lay in a position of all-round defence, which was more or less a circle, in a clearing in an oak wood.

After an hour of rest Fatty woke me: I was on watch. I crawled out of my sleeping bag and into the cold night air. Dark, swirling clouds rolled rapidly across the bright moon. Shivering and with my weapon in the ready position, I was struck by the noise. We were supposed to be silent, but at least one man was snoring loudly, and one was rustling his sleeping bag on the leaves. Another, his lungs congested with phlegm, was coughing, spluttering and sniffling in his sleep. This must have disturbed Spike, for he turned suddenly and whispered in a voice that carried, 'Shut fucking up!'

At five-thirty we patrolled back to the bunker and from there were driven by four-tonners to a river. To pass the river-crossing test, each patrol had to construct a raft out of its bergens in water, and swim silently, in full kit and webbing, with this raft across the river. As we approached the water I could see that it was less than fifty metres wide, but as still and smooth as glass. It was freezing anyway, as one would expect for a Sunday morning in December, but somehow the act of looking at it made it appear colder. Not a single ripple disturbed the mirrored surface. I shuddered at the thought of swimming to the far side and back. No wind blew.

Leafless trees stood silent. No one moved save for a solitary frogman, who stood on the shore.

The most unfortunate man in our patrol was the lead scout, for he had to enter the water first and assemble the raft. He also had to dismantle it on the other side and was, therefore, the last to leave the water. The most fortunate man was tail-end Charlie. He entered the water last and left it first on the other side, to position himself as sentry. Spike nominated Will as lead scout and me as tail-end Charlie.

We were the last patrol to make this double crossing, and by the time we came to the banks to be used, they were as wet and muddy as slippery slides. Will entered the water first and one by one we passed our bergens down the banks. He lashed them together using poles, karabiners and para-cord.

My turn came to join the others in the river. I stepped down onto the sloping bank, the last of thirteen men to go this way, and immediately lost traction. I slipped, accelerated downhill and did not stop until, completely submerged, I hit the bottom of the river. I came up too shocked to swear and gulped in a mouthful of cold air. My skin suddenly tightened like wet rope shrinking around a winch and for a dreadful moment I feared cramp.

We swam, still wearing our cap-comforters, with one hand on the raft and the other sweeping through the water just below the surface. Progress was painfully slow: we had too much drag. Our smocks, trousers and canvas webbing soaked up water like sponges. Our boots hung like bricks on our feet and our raft floated like an iceberg, with the bulk of its mass below the surface. We struggled as wasps struggle to move through syrup.

After what seemed an eternity we reached the other side. I scrambled ashore and went on guard, panting and chilled to the bone. Will dismantled the raft and I lifted the bergens, now almost twice their former weight, onto the top of the bank. We patrolled for another hundred metres before Birch made Will enter the water again for a second assembly. If anything, this crossing was far worse than the first because the water was too deep to stand in to make the raft. Will had to tread water while building it. I dropped straight down the vertical bank and into the icy water. We were off again. Progress was so slow I doubted for a moment that we would make it. Two frogmen in an inflatable dinghy waited expectantly for our failure, but we disappointed them.

We drove into Hereford for lunch. I sat with Avery and Will. Even in warm dry clothing we still shivered. Avery had also been tail-end Charlie in his patrol, but he had been ordered by his PC to maintain sentry duty in the water, which was up to his armpits, until the raft had been dismantled. He tried to hold his weapon above the water line while shaking uncontrollably with cold, not realizing that it would work equally well underwater. Avery told us about the technique he had employed to scale the muddy river bank. He clutched the pistol grip on his weapon, with one finger on the trigger guard, while another man pulled him up by heaving on the end of the barrel. Unfortunately, Birch spotted this Laurel and Hardy act and cut in disbelievingly.

'Avery, what the fuck are you doing? Why are you holding the trigger? Are you trying to blow him away?'

We all smiled, and as I cut into my roast turkey, Will looked at me and said, 'Why are you so fucking polite?'

THE BARRACKS

Men with vocations are different from others.
They have more to lose.

Graham Greene

Birch dropped his smile and stepped out from behind the lectern. As he walked the buckle on his stable-belt flashed silver, like the flick of a knife, in the dim light. He stopped at the front of the stage. 'Why do terrorists like car bombs?'

I volunteered an answer. 'Because you don't have to be present, sir.'

'Good. You can plant a bomb with a timing device and then fuck off. Most terrorists don't like fire-fights.' Birch inhaled and then said, 'If only they fucking did.'

The comment reminded me of the ranges we had used on Camp. I could still visualize the paper men and recall the piercing crack as eighteen marksmen, with automatic weapons, responded to the command 'Rapid Fire'. When we patched the targets the hearts had often gone and the chests were like sieves.

Birch went on to explain the alert states in the barracks and what we should do for each one. At the end of the lecture he took us outside and showed us how to search a vehicle for car bombs. We clustered together on one side of the parade-ground and Birch stood in front of the demonstration vehicle, the OC's Volvo.

'You're looking for something,' he said, bending at the knees, and running his hands around the front near-side wheel arch, 'for a box about the size of a double wall socket. They're sometimes magnetic and stuck on in a hurry. Wheel arches, under the rim, anywhere that's easy, they're all classic places.' He stood up and moved to the bonnet. 'If it's under the wheel arches you may be lucky: the engine takes the blow. You may lose your legs, but nothing else.'

Birch lifted the bonnet and searched the engine. He then dropped into the press-up position and looked under the car. Looking up at us, with his chin inches above the ground and his back rigid, like an axle, he said, 'If you do this just outside Harrods you'll look a right cunt. But better that than a dead one.

'By this time,' he said, after checking the underside of the car, 'anyone who's seen you has probably phoned the police.' He stood up, rubbed the grit from his hands, and walked around the front of the car to the driver's door, all the time looking in through the windscreen and the windows. 'When you're absolutely sure, put the key in the lock and turn it very carefully. If nothing happens, put your fingers in your ears and wait for the bang.'

The door swung open and Birch grinned at us, over the roof of the car.

'Any questions?'

At this moment the OC appeared, glancing proprietorially at the blunt, squat car.

'OK, lads,' he said. 'You've done your swimming. We're going to Salisbury Plain this weekend. There's going to be a lot of digging so bring your entrenching tools. You'll be making and concealing an NBC shelter. In times of war you could be stuck down there for several weeks, so they've got to be bloody good. When you come out, you'll be on your own in a toxic environment. It's sabotage and destruction then, lads. It's a tough weekend. You'll enjoy it.'

When the OC had finished bouncing up and down, we walked across the barrack-square and into the locker room. It was a few days before Christmas.

'I got the push this afternoon,' Avery said, opening his locker. He smiled, pleased that, suitably stunned, we had stopped what we were doing.

'Why?' I asked.

'My manager called me in. I thought he was going to tell me about my winter promotion. Instead he told me how some people gave their lives to his sodding bank. "Commitment, Avery, have you ever thought about that?" I thought, oh fuck, here we go.'

'What did you say?'

'I said, "I thought extra-curricular activities were encouraged," and he said, "Nothing conflicts with your work, Avery." '

'What a bastard,' said Cordwell.

'He gave me three days. I've got to be out on Friday.'

'Bastards,' rejoined Cordwell.

'You'll be all right,' said Brown, unlacing his boots. 'You'll easily get another job.'

'I don't know I want one,' he said.

'Your job's got to come first.' Fowkes was shoving his military clothes into his locker.

'Why?'

Fowkes ignored Avery and went on. 'I spent two years building up my business and I'm fucked if I'm letting it go now.'

'Shut up, Fowkes,' said Cordwell. 'We've heard enough about you and your fucking business.' Cordwell stood, stripped to the waist, in the middle of the small corridor dividing the two rows of lockers. He sucked in air like a pair of bellows and, when he inhaled, his ribs rose, stretching his tanned skin. He ignored Fowkes and, looking at Avery, said, 'What about your bonus?'

'I don't know,' said Avery. 'We've done well this year. I'd better fucking get it.'

'How much is it worth?' Cordwell persisted.

Avery hesitated. 'About forty to fifty thousand.'

Sampson spoke first. 'You're fucking mad. You gave up fifty thousand, for this? You're mad, fucking mad.'

'You don't understand,' said Avery.

MOTIVES

The parrot wipes its beak although it is clean.

Pascal

At eleven o'clock in the evening when I had expected to be asleep under cover I found myself in a hole ten to twelve feet deep swinging a pickaxe into white chalk. Our aim was to construct an underground shelter that would protect us from nuclear dust, and known chemical and biological agents. We had forty-eight hours to dig the hole, build the shelter, dismantle it, and fill the hole in again.

It was a crisp Friday night and the first weekend in January. We stood somewhere on Salisbury Plain and the downs extended in all directions, undulating until they faded in the darkness.

We dug by lights powered by a mobile generator and in shifts, one patrol at a time. Will suggested we go first. We chipped away at the sides and scraped the bottom flat. Twelve feet down the chalk was as solid as rock. It was, however, dry and would flake away if struck correctly with a pickaxe. By midnight I was wearing only my running singlet to cover my chest. Two sizes of shovel were available: a man's size and a boy's. Hacking out a shovelful of compressed chalk and then chucking it over a twelve-foot ridge into a neat pile was back-breaking. Eventually someone in another patrol persuaded the Storeman to give us some Chinese buckets to haul the spoil up the sides. Our shift ended just after midnight.

As I stepped off the aluminium ladder at the top of the hole I saw before me an extraordinary scene, one that reminded me of Van Gogh's dark and grubby 'Potato Eaters'. It was a black but starry night. No rain fell but it was very cold. Four rusty posts marked off the site and between these a few dim light bulbs were hung. A diesel generator chugged noisily in the distance. Forty tons of dry, white chalk lay adjacent to the hole, reflecting the moonlight. Standing around this spoil were men steaming, some in soiled T-shirts and others in wet army shirts, their bodies shining with sweat in the half-light. Shovels clanked and Chinese buckets were hauled up onto the heap. Crude jokes were told in small circles as groups stood around watching and resting on their shovels. It was a happy scene. In times of war it would be a desperate one.

A seldom used tank track skirted the hole we were digging and disappeared over the brow of the hill. The topsoil had been scored by the caterpillar tracks and the white chalk lay exposed. The pair of parallel lines rose and fell over the downs, lolloping like a drunken man into the distance. A group of young sycamore trees grew in the incult strip of land on the far side of the track, and we built our bashas there.

When my turn to keep guard came, I stood on the track running in front of the trees and walked quietly up and down. Birch came up to me.

'You on watch?'

'Yes, sir.'

An awkward pause followed. Together we searched the sky in silence. The moon was half full and shining brightly. I thought of Hassan, the stars transporting me to another world and another set of values. But what was Birch thinking? We stood alongside each other and for a while said nothing. Strangely, I felt sure that Birch wanted to talk. But what about? His sheer size made me uneasy.

'Do you ever have a day off?' I said quickly.

'Two weekends a month, but it must be worse for you. A hard weekend and then back to work.'

'Have you always been in the army?' I was relieved that he had answered.

'I joined as a boy soldier at fifteen and passed Selection when I was twenty-one. I knew I was odd and I wanted to do something odd. This regiment suits me.'

Birch continued to talk, but I failed to hear the rest. I had suspected university and Avery had suggested the Guards. If he had said he had a degree in Engineering, I would have believed him: he was informed, eloquent and articulate. But a boy soldier, this was scarcely credible.

'What do you think of the TA?'

'When they sent me here I thought, fucking hell, what have I done to deserve this? But I'm impressed by the commitment. You blokes have got jobs to do as well. It must be fucking difficult. I'm surprised you want to do it.'

'Avery's just lost his job.'

'Has he?' Birch stood six or seven inches taller than me and, looking away, scanned the four-tonners parked among the trees. 'You've got some dedicated blokes here.'

'You must find it frustrating though?'

'Fuck yes. There's not enough time to do anything properly. I took the live-firing weekend on the last course, and at the end of forty-eight hours they were excellent . . . Fours moving aggressively in fucking good formation. But then the weekend's over and you don't do it again for another couple of months. You can't build on it.'

I said nothing. It was Birch, looking back at me, who kept the conversation going.

'I've certainly revised my opinion of the TA. You've got some very bright blokes. Often I have to explain things several times to the regular army. You lot get it first time.'

'It doesn't feel like that, sir.'

'You've done Selection, you're OK. It's the fucking Storeman and all the support staff associated with this regiment that pisses me off. It's a fucking disgrace. They don't do Selection. If anyone saw your Storeman in the field, and he was wearing his beret, they'd say, "Jesus Christ, what's happened to the SAS?"'

We walked towards the brow of the hill without speaking. Birch strode down the middle of the track and I found myself walking alongside, in one of the sunken grooves.

'What do you do in Civvy Street?' he asked.

The quaintness took me off guard. Birch had spent the whole of his adult life shielded from civilians. In a few years he would be entering this world, and it was a world about which he knew nothing at first hand. Soon he would be competing not against soldiers but against civilians, for a job. He began to ask me searching questions about management, but I could not help him. I felt a fraud. Beneath this educated exterior was a man worried about the future. Here was a man, more confident and professional in his job than any I had met, asking me about his next twenty years of employment. I struggled to say something helpful, but I floundered and failed. Fortunately Will relieved me: my watch was over.

Birch went for a walk in the moonlight and I stretched out in my sleeping bag on the wet leaves, but after our conversation I did not sleep easily. For some time into the night I could hear Birch walking quietly around in the copse. I felt I had let him down.

At first light we drew our rations from the Storeman, who slept on the back of the four-tonner jealously guarding his supplies. He was loath to give us anything that might reduce our discomfort. Stores, as far as he was concerned, were best kept safely in the storeroom. He had new rations for us, but he was not going to give them away easily, and only when Birch bawled at him did he reluctantly hand them over. Pleased with ourselves for yet again defeating him, we sat on clods of chalk around the hole and explored the new ration boxes with intense interest. We found not tins of bacon burgers and beans but sealed bags of food that were cooked by placing them in boiling water for seven to eight minutes. The variety was in itself cause for celebration, but when a few had eaten these choice rations they were jubilant. Sampson joined us and said, 'You should try them. They're fucking lovely.'

At eight o'clock we were in the hole again. Before construction of the shelter could begin we had a lot more digging to do. It was hard, strenuous work. Frequently great clods of solid chalk fell on our arms and heads. Grey cumulus clouds rolled through the sky and before long a light rain began to fall. Will looked at me through the drizzle, his grimy face showing signs of fatigue, and said, 'I used to dig in the garden as a boy. Fucking loved it.'

We did not stop until three o'clock in the afternoon, when Gordon brewed some tea. All afternoon we dug on, active, hot, sweaty and jovial. Even the construction was difficult. Two feet below ground level we had left a ledge, and across this ledge we laid pine logs side by side, so that it looked from the outside like an old-fashioned elephant trap in a *Boys' Own* annual. At seven o'clock, we began to shovel eighteen inches of the now wet chalk on top of this. In theory, although we did not do this, the site would be returfed save for the entrance, and the forty tons of spoil similarly camouflaged, so that the disturbance would be invisible from above.

The following morning I got up, aching all over, with the reveille call. The whole patrol shared one mug of tea and began work rather abruptly an hour later. Before we could remove the logs we had to remove the chalk lying on top of them, and doing this was worse than digging the hole in the first place. Not only were we tired and strained from yesterday's labours, but the rain had settled and cemented the chalk.

Once the logs were out, forty tons of congealed chalk lay between us and more rest. Hard work for fit men, but we were suffering from stiff backs. I was used to a heavy bergen, blisters and a bounding pulse, but not to muscle fatigue. We were a comical spectacle, a gang of Walt Disney dwarfs, as we shovelled, picked and sang. By six o'clock on Sunday evening we were sitting around the generator lights in steady rain, having done our bit to returf a tiny portion of Salisbury Plain. We had not concealed our site perfectly but Salisbury Plain, when viewed carefully, is an irregular place. Our turfing too was not skilled, but all Birch said, laconically, was, 'That'll do.'

'What does it feel like to be unemployed?' Avery and I were sitting in his car, waiting for the traffic lights to change, at the end of Buckingham Palace Road.

'It's great,' he said. 'I can spend my whole day at the Gun Club. Got to drill early tonight. I've never had so much time.' Avery sat right back in the GTI, with one hand on the top of the steering wheel and the other on the gear stick. The lights changed and we screeched forwards, skirting St James's Park.

'Have you told your parents?'

'No,' he said. 'My father's bound to be disappointed. He's friendly with one of the directors.'

'Does he know what you're doing?'

'No. I'll have to tell him now.'

'Will he understand?'

'I hope so.' Avery smirked. 'He was a corporal in the Intelligence Corps during the war, so he might. Anyway, I wanted to do something I could respect. Of all the people I used to work with, only two or three were better than me. I couldn't respect the others. They wouldn't have a fucking chance on this course. How's your job going anyway?'

'Grim,' I said. 'Last Thursday the senior partner called me in. I half expected it, so at least I was prepared. He started by saying, "How are you finding things?" You know how it is. They always ask you what you think. They can't come straight out with it. Basically, he said it's proving difficult to find me assignments that are compatible with the TA.'

'Does he know what you're doing?'

'No. If I told him, it would be a lot easier. I told him I was doing a course with the TA, that I had already invested well over a year in it, and that in six months it would be all over. But that seemed to upset him. He went to Eton and plays the cello. I think he's a pacifist. It's a losing battle. I even reminded him that I had checked with personnel, on his advice, before I joined the TA.' We turned onto the Embankment and the lights of the South Bank flickered in the Thames. 'There's a plaque in our foyer signed by the Defence Secretary. It effectively says: this firm supports the Territorial Army. It's a joke. They can't, and they know they can't. It's all pretence. It's incompatible with the work we do. We're expected to move around all the time and if you're in the TA you've got to be at the barracks every week.'

We swung into Red Lion Square and Avery parked the car.

'Let me show you what I bought with my bonus,' he said. He opened the boot and lifted out a radio-controlled jeep. I burst out laughing. Avery bent down and put the jeep in the quiet square. His wiry hair looked almost ginger in the glare of the street light.

'Whatever made you buy that?'

'I was fed up. They were on offer, so I bought it the day I left work.'

He switched the control panel on and we watched the toy car swerve into a greasy hamburger wrapper. It went on and punched a broken polystyrene cup before getting stuck on a drain cover.

'I had a chat with Birch on the last weekend,' I said.

Avery revved his jeep.

'He said he joined the army as a boy soldier when he was fifteen.'

'Fucking hell, that is a surprise.'

'I can't help comparing Birch with the people I work with.'

'He'd never fit in,' said Avery, as we walked over to the drain. 'He's too fucking good. He'd never cope with all the crap.'

'But when he gets to forty-five, that's it. What's he going to do?'

'Fuck knows.' Avery picked his jeep out of the slots in the cover. 'Since he started teaching us I lost what little respect I had for the people at work. Birch is in a different league. I don't think I could ever go back, not now.'

'What will you do?'

'I don't know yet. I'd like to spend a lot more time with 21. There's some fucking good courses if you get through. I couldn't do them if I was working. Most men in the regiment are either self-employed or they work part-time.

'Which is your place?' Avery asked, picking up his jeep.

'This one. Do you fancy a drink?' We went upstairs and entered my flat.

'Are all these your books?' Avery asked, putting his new toy on the carpet.

'Yes. I'm re-reading *Worlds Apart* at the moment: it's by Gavin Young. Do you know it?'

'No. I don't read much any more. I haven't got time.'

'There's a good sketch of David Stirling in there. Look up "Drinks with the Colonel". Like a beer?'

'Thanks.'

We sat down in the armchairs with our drinks, Avery quickly tiring of the book. 'You know,' he said, 'One Squadron is the most educated in the British Army.'

'Who told you that?'

'It's always been the case.'

'I can't believe that.'

'Look at us now. We've got five degrees between the six of us.'

'Do you find yourself more tired since you started doing this?' I asked.

'I'm not too bad, but I don't train as hard as you.'

'That's not what I meant. Aren't you tired of pushing yourself? It's always a hundred per cent. I'm not used to it.'

Avery laughed. 'That's civilian life for you.'

'Do you think you've changed much over the last year or eighteen months?' I continued. 'I mean, besides becoming more aggressive.'

'Yes.'

'Does it worry you?'

'No. Should it?'

'Perhaps it's the effect of Birch,' I said. 'I lose patience a lot more quickly now. I expect people to operate like we do. And they don't.'

From the back of his chair, Avery said, 'I don't bother with civilians any more. All my friends are either in the army or have just left.' He drank the remainder of his beer and picked up the control box for his jeep. 'Would you like to do this full-time?'

'I don't know. I have thought about it. I suppose what worries me is that I'm now neither civilian nor soldier. I can understand Fowkes' comment, that the Paras want to fight. A year ago I thought he was joking, but I can see it now.' The street light shone through the window, casting long shadows across the room.

Avery revved up the jeep and watched it shoot across the floor. 'What do you want to do?' he said. 'Go to war?'

MAPS AND CHEMICALS

Fear death when there is no danger, and not
when there is, for one must be a man.

                                        Pascal

On the Friday night before our next weekend I went to see the
Storeman for a new NBC suit. The one he had given me the
previous weekend was ridiculously large.

'Fuck off and put it on,' he said, crouching down and rummag-
ing behind his counter.

I stepped into the suit and showed him the voluminous, almost
clown-like trousers. He stood up and, with one arm on his counter,
sighed like a shopkeeper who has been asked for an inexpensive
item at the very back of his stores.

'I suppose,' he said, retrieving the small-sized trousers from his
plentiful supply, 'that we have turned you into a lean, fighting
machine.' He threw me the trousers. 'Don't come back again.
They don't come any smaller.'

At one o'clock in the morning we were back in bunker XX and
I was on watch with Brown until two. Standing around in the wet
and cold is always a good prelude to sleep and before long Brown
and I were yawning. We chatted away, hoping to make the time
pass more quickly.

A muddy track ran for five or six miles around the training
ground. Off this a narrow path cut its way through the hillside to
our concealed bunker. Two Land Rovers and the Storeman's four-

tonner had been parked on the outside of the embankment. They stood at the junction of the path and the circuitous track. On the far side of the bunker some scrub land rose upwards, before giving way to woodlands. A disused railway, with a variety of training uses, wound its way around the hillside.

Brown and I stood at the junction, peering across the concave terrain, searching for movement, a change in light, or a change in shadow.

I said, 'Have you seen the jeep Avery bought with his bonus?'

'Yes,' said Brown. He wore a thick shirt, a woollen jumper and a smock. His webbing was neat and tight. He had sewn the camouflaged pouches together so that they were as firm as a set of subaqua weights. During the night he wore his own black, woollen cap-comforter, rather than the issued green one. He was a big man and when he talked to me his head hung forwards like a flower drooping in the wind. He pursed his lips, as if they too were drawn towards the ground. 'I thought I knew Avery, but he's changed a lot now.'

Brown took a step towards the shadow of the Land Rover. 'He's easily influenced by other people. It's been happening for years. I could see the change in our old unit, but it's a lot more obvious now.'

I followed Brown into the shadow and said, 'He spends his whole time shooting, watching war videos and doing this. And he goes to self-defence classes. It's bound to have an effect.'

Brown bent forwards and looked in through the dirty windows at the back of the Land Rover. 'You're right,' he said. 'But it's more than that. It's because it's the SAS and it's supposed to be special.'

'Do you think it's gone to his head?'

We walked around to the front of the Land Rover and stared at the light flickering in the farmhouse in the distance. It started raining and the moon was soon lost in cloud. 'I know what you mean,' said Brown, wiping the raindrops from his eyes. 'You lose a sense of perspective. You've got to keep things in balance.'

'You'd think he'd notice the change in himself,' I said. 'I tried to tell him last week how I thought I'd changed, but he wasn't interested.'

'How have you changed?' Brown asked.

We moved to the leeward side of the four-tonner and stood out of the rain. The tall, dark, canvas roof towered oppressively behind us.

'We go through all this,' I said, 'and do all the training, but then we do nothing with it. It's like training for a race you never run.'

'If there was a war I'd volunteer,' said Brown. 'That would give them something to talk about in the office.'

We moved back out into the rain and away from the vehicles. One or two sheep cried in the distance. The light in the farmhouse was switched off and the training ground went black. Way over to our left the radio aerials soared up into the sky. Even then intelligence was being gathered and messages decoded.

'What concerns me,' I said, 'is that the more we do this, the less useful we are for anything. We're not regular soldiers and we're not successful civilians. If we were, we wouldn't be here.'

'I don't agree,' said Brown. 'We're more successful civilians because we do this as well. We've got more to offer than being just soldiers. We're not regular, but a lot of the regulars couldn't do this and do the sort of jobs we do as well. We'll never be as slick as the regulars because we don't train as much, but that doesn't mean our contribution is less.' Brown put his weapon on the bonnet of the Land Rover and urinated onto the track. The warm water splashed as it fell into a puddle, and the steam rose in the cold rain. 'This regiment was founded on wit and originality,' he said, shaking himself. 'Most of the original members joined up because there was a war on, not because they were professional soldiers.' He did up his trousers and said, 'It was the great spirit of amateurism that made this regiment what it is.'

Brown lifted his weapon off the bonnet and we walked back to the junction. We stood in silence for some time, looking repeatedly at our watches, wishing that the hour would pass and that the next pair would relieve us.

'What do you think of Avery giving up his job?'

'It's a hard decision,' said Brown, 'but it's like the OC said, you've got to make them.'

'Would you give up your job?'

'Now I would. I wouldn't have done until I got through Camp. What about you?'

'Yes,' I said. 'I may well have to.'

Brown smiled, the thick skin on his cheeks looking deathly white against the black of his headgear. 'This regiment's full of misfits. That's what I like about it.'

The second bergen run began at dawn. It was slightly different from the previous runs in that our loads were heavier and, by way of a treat, we could sling our weapons. I guessed that our webbing would neither be checked nor weighed and so removed my two full water-bottles. Luckily, I guessed correctly.

To start with I found myself at the back, but the group quickly spread out as Birch leapt effortlessly like a gazelle along the winding track. I made my way through the gaps up to the front where I met Fowkes. I tried with great difficulty to keep pace with Birch. When we eventually returned to the bunker Birch stood upright, not at all out of breath, and made a mental note of the late arrivals. He said nothing but his stare was worse than a mouthful of abuse. Only when the last man came in did we unstrap our weapons and lift off our bergens.

Birch lectured all morning, in the dark and dank bunker, on map-making and camouflaging observation posts. His confident, easy style fascinated me. Birch was neither flighty nor consciously elegant. He was astonishingly alert and his message was clear and concise. He wasted neither words nor energy and yet he spoke effortlessly, without notes, and with humour. The message was not open to dispute: 'The SAS do things this way because, having tried and tested the alternatives, this one has proved to be the best.'

Birch showed us maps and technical drawings that he and others in the SAS had produced. He passed around cross-sections of bridges, plans of military encampments and diagrams of power stations. They were professionally produced in ink and in colour, with clearly marked dimensions. The stress points had been marked with black arrows and these fascinated Avery. Each diagram came with a folder of supporting documentation. They had been produced by SAS soldiers, working, often behind enemy lines, like clandestine gymnasts, with tape measures and notebooks. The best attire for such operations was not combat clothing but black tracksuits and plimsolls. Such operations require stealthy, silent movement, both on the ground and in water. The purpose of such diagrams is to facilitate rapid and effective demolition.

Accompanying each diagram were several maps of the surrounding area, all drawn to different scales and focusing on different features. One map included the course and direction of rivers and streams, and the types of woods: coniferous or deciduous. Another included the layout of buildings, the location of doors, lights and cables, the position of guards and a note on the frequency with which they changed. The detail and the accuracy of the information was remarkable, but Birch went on to explain that a map produced by one patrol might ultimately be used by another, sometimes days or even years later. And a man about to risk his life wants to know as much about the terrain and the escape routes as possible.

The lecture lasted for several hours. We were told that we would be practising during the night what we had learned during the day. Each patrol was to be split in two. One half would spend part of the night preparing a map and the second half would, before first light, test the map with a simulated attack.

Before the production of a map could begin, however, the terrain in question would have to be watched for days, sometimes weeks or even months beforehand, to ensure that it was safe to begin. To this end, after lunch, and in pairs, we were ordered to construct observation posts, such as a trench or a camouflaged nest in a hedgerow.

Birch put Fowkes and me in a pair and instantly created a problem. Having been in the Parachute Regiment, Fowkes had an acquired dread of digging, whereas I had always enjoyed it. As a child I liked nothing better than to dig in the sand. I liked to dig huge holes; holes so deep that when I stood in them my head was below ground level. I used to dig down until I struck rock or even the water table. If I was lucky this was very deep. Digging up pebbles or big stones was the best bit; the bigger the stone the more fun I had. This was not a purely physical endeavour. It was highly technical, for at five years of age I knew that if I dug too close to the sea I would reach the water table too quickly, and yet, if I dug too far away, the soft, dry sand would always slide back into the hole. The site, therefore, was critical to success. And so it is with an observation post.

Fowkes and I compromised and did not dig. Instead we made a nest in a bush. Unfortunately it was so well camouflaged that when inside we could observe nothing. Also it was very hot for we had an eiderdown of canvas, turf and pine needles on top of us. But Birch was complimentary when he found it after much scrambling around the woods.

Two hours later Spike gave us our orders for the night's activity. We were to map the area immediately surrounding a howitzer. The other patrols had been given different features in the training area. Avery's patrol was given the task of mapping the area immediately surrounding a derelict railway station. We had been pitted against the OC: he was going to sit on top of the gun. If he saw us, we knew there would be trouble.

I was lead scout which meant that I carried the patrol's only night-viewing aids. Jim, Spike and I formed the recce party and it was our job to sketch the map. To do this without being seen by the OC was a daunting task: he had eyes like an owl's at night. Will, Gordon and Fatty stayed with the bergens at an RV overlooking the gun.

Unfortunately a shallow ditch ran through a field more or less from the RV up to the howitzer and around to the side. Spike wanted us to crawl up this ditch, around to the back of the gun and, from there, emerge into scrubland. Once in the scrub we could examine and map the land, by moving, crawling and climbing as necessary. What Spike did not know was that the ditch was full of water, polythene, broken glass and tangled brambles.

We crawled along the ditch. Through my night-sight, I could see the OC scanning the fields keenly. The rain had eased off some time ago. The trees stood still: no wind rustled their branches. If we made any noise, the OC would hear us. The weather was not on our side. Even the moon illuminated the fields either side of the ditch. We would have to stay in shadow. I longed for mist and strong wind, anything to conceal our movement.

The three of us wriggled along the ditch on our stomachs. When I stopped at an obstacle, Spike whispered at my feet, 'Keep fucking moving.'

I rolled onto my side and, looking back at him, pointed to a dense hawthorn bush growing up out of the ditch.

Spike rolled his eyes and said, 'Get up and go round it. Fucking hell!'

I crawled out of the shadow of the ditch and into the moonlit field. For a few seconds I was in what felt like broad daylight. I lay on my stomach out of cover, and in full view of the OC. Rarely had I felt so exposed. I could even feel the gods slapping my back: 'Come on, your time is up.' Suddenly a shot pierced the silence and I launched myself back into cover in front of the hawthorn. I lay as still and as silent as a frightened cat. Only my breathing disturbed my ears. A few minutes later I carefully raised my weapon and focused the night-sight on the OC. He had his back to me. He had fired at another patrol. We had not been seen.

Jim and I spent the next few hours exploring and carefully mapping the area. Spike hid at a safe distance and watched our dexterity. I always kept at least one eye on the OC. When the operation was complete we returned by a different route, crawling on our stomachs through two hundred yards of sheep dung behind a small ridge to the RV. When we met the others we were drenched with sweat. Having not moved for three hours they were rigid with cold. Sweaty and soiled with dung, we were back in the bunker by two o'clock and our map, which was noticeably inferior to the ones Birch had shown us, was ready within an hour. Sleep came easily.

Will kicked me in the legs at ten minutes to four. I jumped up, and looked at him fiercely. I was on watch at four. It was an unforgivable sin to wake a man unnecessarily early for watch. 'The times have changed,' he said. 'The roster is by the fire. You'll see it.'

I walked over to the fire in the corner. I found the roster and struggled to make sense of the handwriting. My name appeared alongside the entry: '03.50–04.30.' Spike had lit a fire in a rusty oil drum and had left his well-thumbed pornographic magazine on the floor. I dragged one of the mouldy airline seats up to the drum and sat down with my feet on the rim. I picked up the magazine and scanned it somewhat desultorily but at four-fifteen in the morning it hardly helped to pass the time at all. At four-thirty I walked around the damp bunker and woke up the rest of the patrol.

Dirty, clammy and black with a mixture of camouflage cream and sheep dung, the six of us moved back to the RV we had left a few hours earlier. Will, Fatty and Gordon were to attack the howitzer without being seen by the OC. They were to use, and therefore test, our map. Jim and I were to remain at the RV and provide covering fire. The attack began at first light.

Jim and I lay a few feet apart in the frosty grass. At the designated time we opened fire on the howitzer with three hundred blank rounds. The OC immediately dived for cover. Will, Fatty and Gordon moved forwards, from the points of concealment we had marked on our map. They moved within the permitted time frame, which was a matter of seconds, and took possession of the howitzer.

In less than ten minutes the attack was over. Swirling smoke swung transiently around our weapons. Spent cartridges lay in the white frost, glistening in the sunlight. The final hour of darkness had been violent and noisy but suddenly there was peace. Leafless trees cast long shadows and sheep moved out into the sunlight, creating their own little shadows. Ahead of us the sky was a flaming yellow and behind us a dark blue. In minutes the moon and stars were obscured from view. From the crack of automatic fire we moved into the tranquillity of dawn.

'Beautiful, isn't it?' said Jim.

'Yes,' I said, still lying down and looking over my sights and into the frosty grass. 'Yes, it is.' I unclipped my magazine and took the remaining round out of the chamber. 'It's quiet now, too.'

The killing group came back and reported a success. The map had proved, in this rehearsal, adequate. But Spike explained that the emphasis was not so much on the attack, but on an understanding of the procedures required to assimilate data rapidly, and in enemy territory. Demolition was something we would practise if, and only if, we were admitted into the regiment. At this stage we were being exposed to the sort of skills that would, ultimately, be required of us. We were not expected to be proficient in them, but we were expected to demonstrate that with further practice we could become so.

'Good effort,' said Spike at the end of his debrief. 'Let's sit over there and wait for Birch.' We walked over to a purpose-built tower four or five storeys tall, and with the windows removed.

Birch turned up half an hour later with some abseiling kit and five of us spent a happy hour abseiling down the outside of the tower. We were then driven straight to a gas chamber for the rest of the exercise.

I dug deep into my bergen and pulled out my NBC suit, a graphite suit that is supposed to protect against nuclear, biological and chemical weapons. I put the suit over my now stinking smock and just as I was tightening everything up, Spike dropped a smoke grenade at my feet.

'*Gas!*' he shouted.

I had nine seconds to put on my respirator. I closed my eyes, stopped breathing, found the respirator, put it on and shouted '*Gas, Gas, Gas.*' To do so took nine seconds. Spike pushed us into the chamber.

The chamber itself was an old bunker totally sealed from the outside world, except for one or two cracks in the wooden door frame. There was no time to contemplate its sinister overtones. We had a job to do, and that was to explore the interior. Wearing name labels on our chests to identify ourselves, we felt our way around the walls. Dense, swirling red smoke obscured anything more than a foot away from view. Carefully treading our way over the rubble and refuse, we were forever stretching and splaying out our arms for the man in front, just as slugs carefully feel their way in blindness by contracting and expanding across unknown territory. A broken cartwheel, a rotting gate, polystyrene foam, old newspapers, fish-and-chip wrappers, a shop-window mannequin, cow dung, cardboard, broken glass, all this was in our way. We walked slowly, talking to ourselves; for voices do not easily carry through a respirator and in a gas chamber.

Spike stumbled and suddenly burst through the mist, like Magwitch on the marshes. 'Practise changing your canisters,' he bellowed through his respirator into my ear.

A canister is nothing more than a filter on the side of the respirator and its lifespan depends on the environment in which it is worn. In a highly toxic environment a soldier may have to change his canister several times during an exercise. One slip, in a lethal environment, could result in death. The changing procedure is simple: take a deep breath, close your eyes, unscrew the old canister from the respirator, screw on the new canister, breathe out hard and open your eyes. However, great presence of mind is required to remove a failing canister from a respirator in a toxic environment. An even stronger nerve is required to screw on the new canister, without crossing the thread, blind to one's motions and unable to breathe. If the thread gets crossed, and it invariably does, one must stay relaxed and not on any account breathe. To fail to find the thread after two or three attempts and try again, carefully, requires the patience of a saint. We practised in a chamber of concentrated tear gas and that was bad enough. We also practised a number of other drills before being let out.

Once outside I ripped off my respirator and filled my lungs with fresh air. My eyes adjusted slowly to the blinding sunlight. I sat on a dirty concrete step with the others, swinging the rubber face mask from my hand, and stared blankly down into the frozen mud.

Will sat down beside me. 'You all right?'

'Yes.' I wiped the sweat from my face. 'It's depressing, isn't it?'

'What?' Will was looking at the track that ran purposefully away from the gas chamber. The muddy puddles had frozen and a few empty smoke canisters had been trodden into the ground. The warm sun lapped at the mixture of manure and cam cream on our cheeks, and we squinted in the brightness. Our hair was dirty and matted, and the grease shone in the sun. The fields in the distance, on the far side of the training ground, looked clean and white, but they too, when viewed closely, were littered with the rusty casings of explosives and grenades.

'This,' I said. 'These suits . . . On a day like this, too.'

'Yes. Fucking depressing.' Will swung his respirator in his hand. 'It makes me think of the war graves Jim and I went to in the summer.'

I kept in the shade; even the tarmac stretched and softened in the baking sun. The quiet lanes led me through grand residential areas now decrepit, decaying reminders of a presence long gone. A neglected building, its paintwork scorched in the sun; a crumbling gatepost; a pair of wrought-iron gates left open not closed, rusting in the undergrowth. Forgotten flowerpots lining a driveway. A few roses gone wild, now briars.

I arrived at the entrance to the cemetery just as the sun was passing its zenith. Two dark-skinned gardeners, employees of the British Government, sat in the shade of a tree, awake to my presence but too tired to respond. I walked around the manicured lawns alone.

Row upon row of bronze plates converged like railway lines at points in the distance. Each memorial was separated from the next by a small shrub. Plants that might ordinarily grow out of control were here kept respectful, pruned and watered. I read every inscription but the pleasure was painful. Sentences bounced around my head like an echo reverberating around a quarry. *Silent,*

Unseen, he stands by my side whispering, 'Dear wife death cannot divide'
... aged twenty-three ... *Greater love hath no man than this, that a*
man lay down his life for his friends ... aged thirty ... *He died that we*
might live ... aged twenty-four ... *At the going down of the sun and*
in the morning, we will remember them ... aged forty.

Will peered straight into the frosty embankment. 'Depressing ...
Fucking depressing. Everyone should visit them ... They were just
ordinary geezers like you and me. Christ! They just wanted to live
another day, too.'

SHOOTING

You must kill immediately.
SAS Staff Instructor

We returned to the squadron barracks for another two drill nights before the next test weekend. The weekend was to be a straight shooting exercise using some of the Storeman's more obscure and foreign weapons.

During the intervening weeks Birch persevered with the core courses of chemical warfare and first aid, and every week our pile of lecture notes grew. Often Birch would spend the last half-hour of a drill night briefing us for the forthcoming weekend. This time, standing on the stage with the six of us looking up at him from behind our rickety desks, he talked about shooting.

'Remember, you are not shooting at targets. You think of them as guns pointing at you. Every round counts . . . You must kill immediately.' Birch paced across the stage like a restless and confined lion. 'If you get caught in a fire-fight, what do you do?' He stopped in his tracks, like the lion that suddenly sees something move.

'Return fire,' said Fowkes.

Birch laughed. 'That's a start. The British Army teaches a double tap. It's crap. You fucking give it to them. I was in a patrol in the Falklands. When we engaged an enemy patrol we got through four thousand rounds in a couple of minutes.' He paused to let this sink in. The concept of carrying four thousand rounds, between four men, in addition to the normal load, was daunting enough. 'You are shooting to kill,' he continued, 'that's what it's all about.'

Birch began to pace back and forth again across the stage. He stopped in the corner and looked at Cordwell. 'What do you do if one of you gets wounded in a fire-fight?'

Cordwell rolled his pen between his fingers, as if feeling for the answer, and then, with his feet sticking out from under the table, said, 'Would you leave him, sir?'

The smile vanished from Birch's face and for a fraction of a second he was stunned. 'Like fuck you do. When you've seen a wounded man, you'll fucking go and get him.' His eyes flashed as if six bloody men were lying before him. 'You fucking get him.' Birch lowered his voice. 'It tends to spoil the day if you don't.'

That Friday we slept in the barracks. I did not wake until five o'clock the following morning when Avery shone a torch into my eyes.

'Come on,' he said, 'we're off.'

Half an hour later we sat on the ribbed floor of the squadron four-tonner thundering towards the Guards' Depot for the beginning of another weekend. It was the first time we had not travelled on a Friday evening. Instead we drove the fifty miles to the Depot before dawn. I hoped I was in for a treat. Since Camp we had scarcely bothered with drill. We never marched anywhere or saluted officers. We slouched around with our hands in our pockets and called each other by whatever names took our fancy. I was looking forward to seeing some polished drill and shiny boots. I stared sleepily from the back of the four-tonner but could see nothing except the linings of drawn curtains.

Avery shared my disappointment. 'I suppose the Guards get up a little later than us,' he muttered.

As we slowed down at the end of the ranges, Cordwell and Fowkes were finishing their conversation on Selection. The last thing Cordwell said, seconds after we had stopped, was, 'It's interesting the way they got rid of the loudmouths.' At that moment Birch appeared at the back of the four-tonner. He unhooked the tail-gate and looked coldly at Cordwell before addressing us all. 'Come on,' he said, 'out you get.'

When inside military barracks and secure environments Birch always wore his beret, whatever the weather. Unlike our cap-comforters, which had a habit of unfolding themselves, Birch's beret never appeared to move, and neither did I ever see him touch it. It sat on his head more firmly than his hair, for it never blew in the breeze or looked any different whether it was wet or dry.

There was something almost mystical about Birch's appearance; unlike us, he never appeared tired. I never heard him panting after a run, no matter how long or fast it had been. And his dress never deteriorated. Birch could run across a muddy field and emerge clean. Try as we did to emulate him, we always came through worse off, like ragamuffins splattered in mud. Where Birch emerged crisp and tidy, we fell apart. Our pockets fell open, our trousers slipped, our webbing rattled, and our cap-comforters came untucked so that they dangled like nightcaps from our heads. Trying to rise to Birch was a losing battle. It is surprising that we never gave up.

We jumped out of the four-tonner and the six of us joined up with the remaining seven recruits from the other four squadrons. They had already arrived and were busy cleaning their weapons at the end of the ranges. We began shooting with our SA80s at electronic targets as soon as the range warden arrived, but by mid-morning the driving rain had turned to sleet and later on to snow. At that point we began to use our foreign weapons.

We lay on the wet ground in the prone position, with one knee drawn up, and our elbows locked at near right-angles, as we clamped the butts back into our shoulders. The snow fell and our backs were soon white. Only the black of our boots showed through. Icy melt-water ran down our necks and soaked through our thin, porous smocks. Gloves were not permitted, as they were said to restrict sensitivity and firmness of touch. Instead our hands went numb as they clasped, without moving, bitterly cold steel. Our trigger fingers moved an inch each time, but otherwise we remained motionless, the ground drawing at the warmth of our blood.

Soon the targets were lost in the swirling snow and accuracy became difficult.

Each man had at his side three or four foreign weapons to try and we changed from one to the other at Birch's command. The British SA80s were the most difficult of all to fire, for our optic sights misted up every five seconds as the warm air from our faces condensed on the glass. Avery confessed to me that, at a hundred yards, he could not see the target through his lens. His technique was to wipe the glass with his forefinger and rapidly fire a shot, before wiping it again.

When Birch gave the order we laid down the SA80s and picked up Chinese AK47s.

The last time I had seen one of these weapons was in 1986 when I had gone to the North-West Frontier Province of Pakistan. The snows had fallen and I had gone to Garam Chasma on the Pakistan/ Afghan border with an old map printed by the Royal Geographical Society. I had expected to find nothing more than a few hot springs, but when I arrived I discovered not a deserted hill village, but a formidable *ad hoc* military encampment. Hundreds of pack-horses and thousands of ammunition cases littered the small valley. Mujahedin, some wearing Soviet belts, slunk around the piles of supplies, slinging AK47s from their shoulders. Every so often the crack of live fire would echo in the snow-filled valley as someone somewhere let off a few rounds.

Several days after I left Garam Chasma I set out on foot from Mastuj, with the intention of walking to Gilgit. One morning I got up before dawn. A long day lay ahead of me: I was going to walk to Gupis. I picked up my aluminium water-bottle and dropped it instantly. Like dry ice it had stuck to my skin. When it hit the hard ground I could tell by the clunk that it had frozen solid. I struggled in the rarefied air to put on what clothes I had: boots, socks, thick shirt and trousers, leather gloves, woolly hat and a mountaineering jacket. Fully dressed I still felt cold. As I rolled up my sleeping bag in the dark, two men and a boy appeared in the valley, wearing little more than torn cotton trousers and thin, open-necked shirts. They wore rubber boots, much too big for them, no gloves, no socks and certainly not hats or coats. The little boy could not have been a day over six years old. I stared disbelievingly and felt weak. I had not encountered men like this before and their hardiness surprised me.

Remembering these men and the boy as I lay on my stomach in the wet snow, I tried to stop shivering. Even Birch looked cold. Snow clung to his beige beret and he put on a brave face, but we were not hitting much, and he halted the exercise. We stood up, picked up our weapons and sprinted to the four-tonner. I ran behind Cordwell and could see the pouches on his webbing flapping, where he had forgotten to button them down. Birch strode alongside, springing effortlessly like an arctic hare.

'Cordwell,' he said, leaping past him, 'look at your webbing: it's a bag of shit. For fuck's sake, get yourself sorted out.'

A couple of hours later, all thirteen of us returned to the One Squadron barracks. Having aborted the exercise, Birch spent the rest of the weekend going over most of the course work we had learnt to date, in preparation for the written exams at the end. For the first time the other recruits were able to experience Birch's style.

At one point the OC entered the classroom and, having apologized to Birch for the interruption, said, 'Cordwell, this way.' He motioned through the open door. 'Bring your kit.' Cordwell picked up his lecture notes, pushed the plastic chair under his desk, and, without turning round, walked out. The OC nodded at Birch and closed the door.

Birch, still wearing his beret, glanced after them. 'Don't ever get cocky. It doesn't pay. In this regiment a cocky soldier is a hazard: he can get you all killed. You won't see him again.'

For the rest of the afternoon Cordwell's desk remained empty and we continued to revise the drills for urinating and defecating when wearing NBC suits in a toxic environment. 'It's better,' said Birch, smiling, 'if you can, to hold it. If you're lucky, and you're in a nerve-gas environment, you'll decontaminate and change your suits every twenty-four hours.' This was some comfort, for the degree of care and contortion required in a lethal zone, where one slip could result in death, was enough to stop one from ever eating or drinking.

We used confidential textbooks to accompany the chemical warfare course and at the end of this session Avery said, 'I can now see why these books are restricted. If anyone got hold of them we'd be the laughing stock of Europe.'

On Saturday evening we were stood down until seven o'clock on Sunday morning. I persuaded Fowkes and Brown to see *Casualties of War* in Leicester Square. The three of us drove in Fowkes' car.

A long-range recce patrol kidnap a Vietnamese girl and take her along for some rest and recuperation. They rape her, beat her, attempt to stab her and finally shoot her. One member of the patrol refuses to take part. He is shaken beyond belief. He reports his colleagues' actions to his superiors but they are not sympathetic. Life, they say, is different in the combat zone. The lonely man agrees that it is different: it is precarious, one may die any second. One should not, therefore, be reckless and frivolous but extra vigilant, for every moment is important and every action significant.

We emerged from the cinema and walked out onto Shaftesbury Avenue. Brown walked in a cotton jacket, jeans and training shoes. His step was silent. Fowkes strode along in shabby whipcord trousers and a pair of black brogues that were noticeably worn in the heel.

'I'm glad Cordwell's gone,' said Brown. 'It's safer now. He was unbalanced. He had a bad effect on Avery, too.'

'Not many of us left now,' I said. We walked, three abreast, dodging the crowds, down towards Piccadilly Circus. 'What surprises me is the price we all pay, even the losers.'

'It's not worth it,' said Fowkes.

We stepped down into the Underground and emerged on the south side of the statue of Eros. We walked on through the bustling crowds and into a noisy restaurant on the Haymarket.

'You look troubled,' I said, laying down my menu and looking at Fowkes.

'I don't know why I'm on this course,' he said. 'Every time I pick up a weapon, I ask myself, "Why am I doing this?" I joined to get outside, to get out into the hills.'

'But you heard Birch,' I said, 'the aim is to kill. The hill walking's over.'

'I know,' said Fowkes. 'But there's more to life than fucking killing.' He pulled off his jumper and draped it across the back of his chair. Underneath, he wore a creased shirt and the top few buttons were undone. His complexion was hard and his face bony. 'When I left the Paras, I resolved never to pick up a weapon again. Now look at me.'

'You can't resist a challenge.'

But Fowkes ignored my comment and continued. 'I worked as a missionary after the Paras.'

'How did you manage that?'

'My uncle was a missionary in the Philippines. When I finished my catering course in Hong Kong I went out to help him.'

Brown raised his arm and attracted the attention of the waitress. He ordered a large pizza and three beers.

'I remember once,' said Fowkes, 'my uncle went off to conduct a service about twenty miles away. He left me in charge of his church. I'd never taken a service before. It was an incredible experience. The people loved it. They came from miles around. They were chanting and singing: you can't imagine it. It was the first time I felt I'd done something really useful. And now this. It's fucking wrong, Birch telling us we must kill all the time.'

'You're quiet, Brown,' I said.

'I'm listening.' Brown had long legs and was never able to sit comfortably at a small table, unless he could stretch them out. He shuffled and fidgeted, forever searching for a less awkward position. 'I believe in the TA, especially this unit. It's good training for life.'

'And death,' said Fowkes sardonically, lifting the ashtray off our small table and balancing it on the edge of a plant pot.

'I can't help thinking about people like Para, and for that matter, Birch,' I said. 'In many ways Para belongs in the army. He got divorced after the Falklands and now he's unemployed again. At least he had a role here. Now he's got nothing.'

'Yes,' said Brown, 'but the army doesn't exist to provide fulfilment.'

'I know that, but you've got to admit that Para was better off here than on the streets.'

Brown uncrossed and recrossed his feet. His legs stretched out sideways, tangentially, away from the circular table. 'It's not the purpose of the MOD to provide jobs.'

'But what about Birch? What's he going to do when he retires in a few years' time?'

'I don't know,' said Brown. 'He decided to join. He knew he'd have to go at forty-five.'

'So? He's given his life to the army. What do you say when he gets to forty-five, "Tough shit, Birch. Thanks for everything: you're on your own now"?'

Fowkes laughed and the waitress came shuffling across the restaurant with our pizza. It was only when we stopped talking that I realized how noisy and crowded the restaurant was. Behind the laughter and the hum of conversation was the steady clatter of cutlery.

'What do you think will happen to Birch?' asked Fowkes.

'I don't know,' I said. 'He frightens me. There's something awesome about Birch, utterly ruthless. It's the OC's point about the flick of a switch, and you're a different man. But it's not mechanical. What makes it sinister is that he's so intelligent. You saw how he flew at Cordwell.'

'It's self-discipline,' said Brown. 'That's all it is.'

'Doesn't it alarm you, though,' I said, 'when you see that aggression?'

Fowkes cut the pizza into six and began sharing it out.

'There's something tragic about Birch,' I went on, cutting into the food. 'He'll end up like Mr Prewitt in *Brighton Rock*.'

'What's that?' asked Brown.

'Just a nobody at a bus stop.'

We ate in silence for several minutes. It was Fowkes who spoke first.

'It's wrong,' he said, 'I know it's wrong.'

'You might as well see it through, now,' said Brown. 'In two months the course will be over. If you feel that strongly why not get the badge and then go?'

'It's a funny thing,' Fowkes said, still chewing his pizza, 'but my grandfather was in the army. He was a major-general when he retired. He hardly ever talked about war. Only once, when I was about ten, did he tell me about the First World War. He said he was running forwards in a charge, and when he looked up half of them had gone. When he looked again, they'd all gone: he was the only one left standing. He said he fell to the ground and pretended he was dead. He crawled back during the night.'

Fowkes lifted his beer and drank half the glass in one go.

'Was your father in the army?' I asked.

'He was in the Guards.' Fowkes put his glass back on the table. 'He hated it: he bought himself out. He's done very well for himself since.

'You know,' he said, 'if I were you, I'd marry your girlfriend and forget all this.'

Brown caught my eye but said nothing.

'If you leave now, Fowkes,' said Brown, 'you'll never come back.'

'I know,' said Fowkes. 'But there are lots of other things to do in life. If my business fails I'd like to go back to the Philippines.'

SNOWDROPS

Man's sensitivity to little things and insensitivity to the greatest things are marks of a strange disorder.

Pascal

The following morning Fowkes decided to leave us. No one asked him about his conversation with the OC. He left the barracks alone, strong in his own decision, and yet disappointed that he had started something he could not finish.

A fortnight later we returned to Salisbury Plain for the second live-firing weekend. The purpose of this exercise was to rehearse some of the techniques required in close-quarter battle (CQB), or fire-fights in confined spaces. These might be, for example, inside buildings, on aeroplanes, or even in small, compact woods.

It was midnight before the four-tonner stopped with a jolt on a muddy incline, somewhere on Salisbury Plain. A track scarcely big enough for a bicycle disappeared into some trees. As soon as we unloaded our kit, the Storeman reversed the truck back down the track and drove off into the darkness. The four of us picked up our bergens and kit bags and walked the two kilometres to our destination, which was a solitary barn. Birch and the other squadrons were already there.

The barn was large and unkempt. Brushed into the rough concrete was a mixture of manure and straw, hardened, as all manure does with age. A rusty steel framework supported a galvanized metal roof, and the sides were made of sheets of corrugated iron. The metal roof rattled all night in the wind.

Avery and I were on watch from three-fifteen until four o'clock. Brown and Sampson relieved us. At five-thirty I followed Sampson over to the Storeman, who had arrived some time during the night, and collected my rations.

I found a packet of cheese spread that was nine months past its sell-by date. I had once been given a ration pack with bacon burgers that were eight years old. The Storeman's spoiling us, I thought, and ate the cheese eagerly. The new rations, however, did not stay in our systems for very long, and during the morning we discussed the relationship between defecation and ration menus. Such conversation was a favourite topic, for not only did diet affect our morale, but constipation or diarrhoea occasioned by army rations frequently affected our ability to work well.

At first light Birch drove us, in his Land Rover, to a copse at the foot of a valley. One side dropped steeply and the other rose gently with the curve of the downs. The copse was just above the stream at the bottom, on the shallower incline. A track ran straight down the steep side, through the stream and up over the downs, skirting the edge of the trees. The bottom of the valley was broad and flat. The large meanders in the stream, which got lost under the tufts of grass, kept the muddy ground saturated. No chalk was visible here.

It was in this wet, marshy ground that Birch had constructed a practice range. Using lengths of wire and a sequence of pulleys, he was able to control a number of hinged targets that lay concealed in the long grass. The pulleys were welded to long spikes which had been driven deep into the ground, and the wires, which ran down the range, were barely visible.

Falstaff returned for this exercise and he sat, at a safe distance, with a selection of levers like a railwayman in a signal box. When he pulled a lever a target would rise somewhere in the first two hundred yards of the sweeping valley. Sometimes the targets rose in the long grass, sometimes behind rotting trees. Occasionally they lay only a few yards in front of us. Then Falstaff would pull his levers and one would flick up, mockingly, like a jack-in-the-box. Falstaff loved this exercise for he was able to tease us just as a cat plays with its prey. He sat on a collapsible chair with his box of levers, chuckling to himself, like a magician playing with a new toy.

We patrolled two at a time down the range, firing, running and diving for cover whenever a cardboard man showed his face. I practised repeatedly with Brown. Birch trailed me, like a tender box coupled to a steam train, watching my movements, and monitoring my speed of observation and swiftness of response. The OC trailed Brown, shadowing his every step.

Brown and I shouted across the dead ground, always telling each other what we were doing with single-word instructions, such as: '*Fire*', or '*Move*', or, if we were changing a magazine, '*Magazine!*'.

Great care was needed on this range, for when zigzagging through scrub and plunging headlong into cover, it was easy to lose sight of one's partner. Had we strayed into their line of fire, we could easily have died. That was partly why Birch and the OC followed us, but the one thing they did not want to see was hesitancy.

We did not stop until five o'clock, when the light began to fade. Then we moved over to the copse, made white by a blanket of snowdrops, and waited for the Storeman to return with the four-tonner. He came in due course over the brow of the hill and, seeing us, accelerated. The four-tonner plunged down the steep track like a roller coaster in free fall, and came abruptly to a halt in a knee-deep paste of wet clay at the bottom. I looked at Birch, our model of excellence, and his facial expression was priceless. The Storeman was not a popular man at the best of times, but such a display of stupidity was extraordinary, even for the army.

All eleven of us and Birch waded out to the disbelieving Storeman and looked by turns at the damage. The rear axle was submerged. Birch directed the operation, completely ignoring the Storeman. Each man found a slab of metal against which to apply his mass. Up to my knees in oozing wet clay, I strained myself, as did every other man, trying against tremendous odds to move four tons of steel. Our heads hung low and we choked on exhaust fumes. All this time the Storeman spun the wheels idiotically, carelessly flicking sludge everywhere. Soon we were caked. Mud and sweat clung to our faces so that only the whites of our eyes showed through. Sampson was behind me grunting like an ox. Jim was in front and kept muttering, 'Fucking Storeman'. We squelched around in the slush trying desperately to improve our traction. Momentarily the four-tonner toppled and we launched ourselves through the quagmire in case it should fall. With Birch's skill and our brute strength we eventually pushed the four tons of clay-encrusted steel back up the slope the Storeman had so recklessly descended.

Unfortunately by the time we got back to the barn there was no time for dinner, so we cursed the Storeman even more. Instead we set off as a patrol with a few prismatic compasses to find a cache, the size of a milk churn, buried somewhere on Salisbury Plain. Birch had given us accurate instructions as to the location, but retrieving a cache is not always straightforward.

The point of the exercise was to demonstrate the importance of precise navigation. As a patrol working behind enemy lines we would often need to replenish our supplies, both of ammunition and food. One method of doing this is by surreptitiously planting caches that can subsequently be retrieved, usually under the cover of darkness. If a hole is dug, in an attempt to retrieve the cache, in the wrong place, even as little as a yard to the right or the left, valuable time and energy is wasted. And a cache of food and water can mean the difference between life and death.

Jim, anxious for sleep, bent his mind to the task and before long we had retrieved the cache. But, disappointingly, it contained nothing more than a few stones, not even a few tins of bacon burgers years past their sell-by date. We were in our sleeping bags, still splattered ignominiously with mud, by two o'clock in the morning.

My turn for watch came three hours later. I was to keep guard alone until six-thirty. I crawled out of my sleeping bag, like a snake shedding its skin, and onto the cold, wet grass. I fumbled for my boots and laced them in the dark. (We were supposed to wear our boots at all times but, when the chances of getting bumped were remote, I removed them and the quality of my sleep was much improved.) I walked out of the woods and jogged around in the moonlight trying to warm up. I even did a few press-ups to improve my circulation. As I lifted my chin three silhouettes on the skyline caught my attention. I jumped up and reached for my weapon but they did not move. I looked again, but I could not tell if they were moving: they were too far away.

The three silhouettes kept me occupied until six-thirty. Then, when it became light, I saw that I had been tricked by the legs of a broken watch tower.

'Anyone see anything on watch last night?' I asked.

'Yes,' said Will, 'I thought I saw three men, but I couldn't be sure. Then it was Jim's watch, so I thought I'd let him worry about it.'

'Fuck you!' said Jim. 'I spent the whole of my watch wondering what they were.'

After we had patrolled back to the copse of snowdrops, Spike started the morning with a lecture on trip wires and explosives. We sat in the valley, away from the shadow of the trees. Spike knelt down in front of us and explained the workings of all sorts of electrical boxes and plastic explosives.

Before long I could hear church bells in the distance. The sun was shining and the sky was a cobalt blue. As I sat on the edge of the copse I thought about the fields of poppies I had seen as a boy, behind our home; now all too rare.

The Sunday morning bells rang out sublimely across the Plain.

'Ballinger, what's the voltage?' Laid out between Spike's knees was a dismantled box of wires.

'Sorry, staff?'

Brown answered for me. 'Three volts.'

'Your name Ballinger?'

'No, staff,' said Brown.

'Ballinger?'

'Three volts,' I said.

'Did you know that?'

'No, staff.'

I had not been listening. It was June, the sun was shining brightly and the sky was a translucent blue. The bell-ringers were hard at work. I was standing in the aisle in my morning coat: a married man.

The rest of the day was spent on the close-quarter battle range. This time Birch and Falstaff had moved their equipment to the copse and concealed their targets among the trees and the scrub. We fired in pairs, running from tree to tree and launching ourselves into cover.

At the end of our turn Brown sighed and said quietly, 'We're destroying the snowdrops.'

SCAVENGERS

The English peel off the unessentials of modernity very easily – they 'go native' more readily than any Europeans except the Italians; and the more refined their upbringing the quicker the change comes about. There is no disgrace in it. On the contrary, in my opinion it shows a creditable regard for the real things in life at the expense of the artificial.

Colonel P. H. Fawcett, 1924

'Listen in, lads,' the OC said. 'Some of you will know Wood. He was trying to join Two Squadron. He's just been dropped from this course. He had a criminal record. It wouldn't matter, lads, but he said he didn't. That's why we ask you on attestation. It catches up with you eventually. You've got to tell the truth, lads. This regiment does not tolerate liars. When you come back from an exercise we've got to be able to rely on your word. People's lives may depend on it.

'I can't fucking understand it,' he said, hopping across the stage, 'you're dropping like flies. That's three in the last few weeks. I hope I'm not going to lose any more. You fucking go for it: one hundred per cent, all the fucking time. Don't give up. Everyone asks themselves from time to time what the fuck they're doing here. We all do: it's only natural. But don't throw it away, lads. It's an honour to be in this regiment, and a privilege.'

When the OC had finished he began his brief for the weekend exercise.

'It's combat survival this weekend, lads. But it's a teaching weekend. You'll do a lot of combat survival courses when you join the regiment; all we can hope to do in two days is teach you the basics. Remember, lads, we're not trying to turn you into experts overnight. We're just preparing you for your sabre squadrons.

'Saturday morning there will be lectures on skinning, cooking and edible foods. You won't go hungry. We've got rabbits, sheep and a whole fucking farmyard for you to have a go at. In the afternoon you'll be setting traps and building shelters. Sunday we've got an exercise laid on with police tracker dogs. You'll enjoy it.

'We've also got to get through some NBC runs. It's a tight schedule, lads. You've got to be able to run in NBC suits and respirators: it's part of the chemical warfare course. It's tough, but the whole pace of war slows down in a chemical environment. It has to. But you might have to run, and you might have to run fucking fast. I'll be watching you on these. They're tests and you've got to pass them.'

'When I did combat survival,' said Birch, towering above the OC, 'it was a two-week exercise. A couple of us hid in a barn.' Birch grinned broadly. 'The farmer's wife kept bringing us jacket potatoes and chocolates.' He rubbed his lean stomach. 'It was tough. At the end of the fortnight, when we were taken back to the barracks, we met one man who hadn't eaten for days. He kept sniffing the back of the Land Rover. He said he could smell chocolate.' Birch laughed. 'You develop an acute sense of smell when you're hungry.'

We drove to the familiar training ground, with the disused railway, the booby-trapped cars and the concealed bunker. When we arrived it was dark, and the OC led us to a corner that we had not visited before. We jumped out of the Land Rover and onto a track bisecting some woods. On one side of the track, sheets of corrugated iron lay discarded in a ditch, along with a car bonnet and a boxwood garage door. A congealed mound of refuse and rubble lay in a clearing between the trees. Strips of metal and broken window frames protruded from the rubbish pile. Concrete had been slopped on top, binding the waste. Plastic fertilizer sacks, a couple of rotting chairs and a Tesco's shopping trolley had been pushed into the scrub. On the other side of the track, a pile of railway sleepers, black with creosote, lay stacked like pipes. Beyond them, the woods got thicker, before stopping abruptly at the edge of the training ground.

Birch had already arrived and came up to us in the gloom.

'Build your bashas over there, tonight,' he pointed to the woods opposite the rubbish tip. 'Reveille's at five-thirty. Bring your bergens and NBC suits to the station.' He pointed to a station platform at the end of the Land Rover track. 'The OC's got your watch roster.'

'Are you on watch?' Birch asked.

'Yes, sir,' I said. The sleeping bags had stopped rustling and the woods had gone quiet.

We stood together for several minutes before I said, 'Are you married, sir?'

'Yes,' said Birch. 'Are you?'

'No, not yet. I'm getting married in the summer.'

'Will you continue to do this?'

The OC had told us his views on marriage and I hesitated before answering.

'I don't know.'

'There's no stigma attached to going,' said Birch. 'You've got a job to do as well.'

His reply surprised me and it was some time before I asked, 'Have you got any children, sir?'

'Yes,' he said. 'I've got a son. He's at school at the moment. He says he wants to join the army. I'm trying to persuade him not to, but what can I say? My son's already done combat survival. I taught him when he was fourteen. He knows how to search the car now as well.' Birch looked down at me and I could feel his gaze fall like moonlight on the side of my face.

At first light we assembled on the edge of the disused railway.

Birch stood with all our bergens at his feet like a lion surrounded by its kill. He weighed each one and if any bergen failed to pull the needle on his balance beyond thirty-five pounds, he filled it with rocks until it did. We stood around in our respirators, adjusting the rubber straps, so they were not too tight or so loose that they would fall off. Birch weighed his bergen and it came to well over forty pounds. He too put on his respirator and we were off on the first NBC test run.

Nine minutes after getting out of bed we were running with S10 respirators and bergens. Birch set the pace and it was a cruel one. For the first few miles about twelve pairs of feet hit the gravel in unison, but as we turned a sharp bend I could see the track straighten out and climb steadily upwards for about three-quarters of a mile. Birch increased the pace. The OC followed. We tried to do likewise. To lose the pacemaker was tantamount to failure, for one had ultimately to catch up with him to avoid punishment, or worse, being dropped from the course. Such sudden, sustained bursts of acceleration were awful. Staying with Birch was bad enough; trying to catch him was practically impossible. The rhythmic crunch of gravel soon ceased, and the machine began to shake. Little by little a fissure appeared and then a fracture; a steam engine out of touch with its governor. We spluttered, spitted and finally collapsed into a set of disconnected pulleys, a broken force. Avery, who had been behind me, pulled off his respirator and vomited onto the verge. Somebody ran forward to take his place in the ranks. I couldn't be sure who it was. It looked like Will, but there was too much condensation inside my respirator for me to see clearly. Suddenly Birch started to sprint uphill, like a flywheel with too much momentum freeing itself from its axle. We tried desperately to follow him, our rubber face masks filling with phlegm. But as soon as Birch broke the machine he stopped on a tarmac clearing just to the right of the track. He removed his respirator and without prompting we dropped our bergens and did likewise. Sweat and condensation trickled out of the face pieces. Birch watched the latecomers, smiling at each one as they came to him. We stayed on the tarmac for forty-five minutes doing PT and at the end of our punishment, still breathless, Birch paced us with our respirators on back to the railway.

There was no breakfast. Instead Birch killed one of the sheep he had hobbled the night before. He strung it up by its back legs between two trees so that, with its dangling head and front legs, it looked like the Star of David. The blood drained from the neck, the heart pumping it out. He pulled off the head and pelt, like a sticky glove, and then opened the belly. The guts flopped out into a plastic sack on the ground.

'Watch out for the gall bladder.' Birch, in a bloody butcher's apron, put his hand into the carcass and removed a sea-green ball of fluid. He grinned, cut the headless sheep from the trees, slung it onto a portable wooden table and proceeded to chop it into joints.

'I enjoyed that,' said Avery, when later he had perfected the knack of twisting off a chicken's head. 'I've always wanted to do it.'

During the afternoon we sat on logs in the small woods opposite the refuse tip and listened to lectures on edible fungi and natural foods. Birch also showed us how to set a range of traps, some of which would have maimed a rhinoceros. He concluded his series of lectures by taking us around the woods and showing us a number of shelters that had been built previously. There were wigwams made out of parachute silk and burrows in embankments. There were tunnels underground like dank drains and shelters on stilts for swamps.

At dusk we divided the raw meat between our patrols and went off into the woods to try to build shelters like the ones we had seen. Will looked at me and said, 'Who's read *Lord of the Flies*? Ballinger, you can be Ralph. Fatty, you'll have to be Piggy.'

Piggy sat grinning on a log with a rusty tin of raw meat and another tin of sheep entrails. He had found the old paint tins half buried in a peaty bog. The rest of us stood around looking at each other. For a while nothing happened. We had become, as if by order, a Chinese Parliament. Will liked to take control. So did Jim. So did I. It was not a good start. Progress was accordingly slow, haphazard and to some extent directionless. The result was a fitting requiem to *Huckleberry Finn*. Within hours we had become scavengers and tramps, smelling vilely of raw flesh.

Between us we retrieved from the rubbish dump some corrugated iron, the garage door, some fertilizer sacks, one of the armchairs, the Tesco's shopping trolley and a Samantha Fox pin-up, pressed between two cracked sheets of perspex. We used this waste to build a shelter that had, from the outside, an uncanny resemblance to a hovel in a city slum. But that was what we were aiming for: an inconspicuous dwelling where we could survive in times of war, and from which we could infiltrate enemy territory, like urban rats.

Jim started collecting wood for the fire. He found some dry pine logs and brought these back to our muddy basha site. I criticized his choice. Pine, I knew, would spit, crackle and burn too quickly. To keep a good fire burning all night we needed hard wood. Jim apologized. The fire, however, had been his domain, and I had unwittingly offended him. He went off desultorily to look for more and invited me to take over. The others watched as I chopped wood with a large hatchet. By sheer good luck I hit the grain correctly on a solid beech log and it split supremely down the middle. The others noticed and Will declared me an instant celebrity.

I continued to chop wood. Once, in my teens, I had helped a farmer fell a walnut tree. It had been dead for years. He cut off the branches with a chain saw, and then cut the trunk at the base, leaving a huge log four feet long. I spent the whole day splitting the branches, on his instruction, with a felling axe. By the evening everything, except the trunk, had been split. The next day he went to the Races in Cheltenham, and, thinking I would do him a good turn, I set about finishing the work and splitting the trunk. Armed with steel wedges, a sledge-hammer and a sharp felling axe I attacked the four-foot log. It split easily. The grain was fabulous. The core was dark and the outer wood was much paler. In half a day I had converted the solid trunk into a pile of top quality firewood. Only when the Races were over did I discover my error.

The walnut tree had been left standing for three years to dry out. A cabinet maker had been commissioned to turn the trunk into a coffee table for the farmer's wife: a special present for their golden wedding anniversary.

Piggy prepared a stew in the paint tins and we made mattresses by half filling the fertilizer bags with wet oak leaves and tying the tops with wire. Our sleeping bags had been confiscated and none of us had any intention of lying on damp ground if we could avoid it.

When we had nearly finished, Birch paid us a visit. We had taken liberties with the exercise and had constructed a four-man basha, outside of which was an armchair for the man on watch. He could sit by the fire and keep it burning. Depending on his inclination, he could either study the stars or stare at Samantha Fox, now hanging indiscreetly from the tree against which our basha was built. To us, this was not combat survival, but the building of a boys' den. When Birch saw the result of our efforts he laughed at our ingenuity, and our cheek. Just as he was about to go, Jim came jogging through the woods pushing the shopping trolley. It was loaded like a wheelbarrow with firewood.

Birch just managed 'Fucking hell!' before leaving us. It was as if combat survival had never been so ridiculous, that a Special Forces patrol had become a teenage rabble in a matter of hours.

We lit our pre-built fire and it burned well. Piggy had secreted some lamb casserole powder in his smock, and now that Birch was safely out of sight he added this to his concoction in the paint tin. I suspended the tin from a branch and it soon bubbled exquisitely like the witches' gruel in *Macbeth*. The five of us sat around the fire, filthy in our soiled clothes and smeared in a paste of sweat and mud, waiting for Piggy to declare the soup done. Only Gordon refused to go near it.

My turn to keep watch came at three in the morning. That night, sitting by the warmth of the fire, time passed almost too quickly. I stared at the burning logs, and the dance of fire on four men's cheeks.

*

When we came back from the bazaar Hassan's daughter was asleep on a rush mat. He picked her up by an arm and a leg so that her other two limbs hung freely. He carefully placed her against the back wall so that there was room for us to sit on the small mat. The sun was just touching the horizon and the colours were smeared like blood on glass.

Hassan's wife cooked. I watched her, through the open door, move around the small communal yard. She stood on a stone, and bent down to the water pipe, to fill a basin with water. The pipe stopped a few inches above the ground. A rusty screw thread on the end indicated that there had once been a tap or a pump, but that had been stolen long ago. Now, the pipe had been bent so that the water trickled out into a shallow ditch. Tin, cardboard, plastic and cigarette packets had been trodden into the earthen yard.

She brought the basin of water inside, added two potatoes and placed the pan over a small dung fire in the corner.

We shared the potatoes and passed around the same cup of water. Hassan woke his daughter and pushed a little potato into her mouth. Seconds later her bowels gave way and she started to cry.

'You should go home, sir,' Hassan said. 'There is nothing for you here. Those men, yesterday, they call you bastard, monkey . . . Crazy men, sir. They hate you. It's not safe for you here now.'

I could easily see the men and the man with the eye but no pupil. He lifted his bundle of rags, and, pulling them aside, left a home-made gun pointing at my chest. I stood inches from the end, silent and empty.

Hassan shouted at them, but I understood nothing and the men did not listen. The trigger was squeezed: the gunman did not hesitate. It was over in a few seconds. Hassan was silenced. But there was no explosion: the working parts just clunked forwards. The chamber had been empty. Hassan looked at me stunned: I had not collapsed.

But then when we walked away, back along the bay, the gunman's laughter followed us, mockingly, over the sands, rolling and tumbling with the curl of the waves, always returning, like the swing back and forth of a restless sea.

'If you want to go, sir, we will go.' Hassan had tried to reassure me. 'I am not afraid to fight and I am not afraid to die. Bangladesh is my country. I am a Muslim man.'

When I woke in the morning Gordon, who was still on watch, had let the fire all but burn out. Will was furious. With considerable difficulty, and with some hot embers and dry twigs, the rest of us resurrected it. As we sat on the leaves waiting for some water to boil, Will turned to me and said, 'Is it true Avery gave up fifty thousand a year to do this?'

'Yes,' I said.

'He's stupid,' said Gordon. 'I've got a wife at home and a daughter. I couldn't give up my job. I wouldn't want to, not for this. It's only a hobby.'

A BIT OF EVERYTHING

When a soldier complains of his hard life try giving him nothing to do.

Pascal

Back at the barracks, on our next drill night, I found the Storeman. He was a plump, verbose man with curly grey hair. Possibly he was once angelic, but twenty-five years in the stores had left their mark.

He looked at me and said, 'What do you want, you pimp? What are you?'

'A new bergen strap, please,' I said. 'This one's broken.'

'See the storeman,' he replied.

'But you are the Storeman.'

'Not any more. There's a new one. Go on . . . Piss off.'

I wandered off and eventually found the new storeman.

'What do you want?' he asked aggressively.

'A new bergen strap, please.'

'Fuck off.'

That evening we assembled in the classroom for the last of the lectures on the core courses. At the end of the session Birch addressed us. 'The end of the course is in sight now,' he said. 'I'm going to take down your hat sizes. If you don't want a beret don't answer.' He grinned with pure pleasure, like a man who had the power to be both benevolent and cruel. 'Any questions?'

But before anyone could answer the OC came into the class-

room. He closed the door and waited in silence, but none of us
spoke to Birch.

'Right, lads,' he said, taking over and still standing in front of the
door. 'You're coming up to the last weekend on the hills.
Selection's a long road, lads. Don't throw it away now. You'll be
doing a bit of everything this weekend. The purpose is to bring it
all together and to show you the sort of things you'll be doing in
your sabre squadrons. There'll be patrolling, an NBC exercise, a
river crossing, a night ambush and an attack using pre-drawn maps.
Concentrate, lads, and listen carefully to everything you're told. I
don't want to be interviewing anyone on Sunday morning.
There's no excuse for failing now.

'The weekend after, it's the badging ceremony. The Colonel
will be here and I want to see some smart haircuts and a fucking
good turn out. Don't let yourselves down now, lads.'

The following Friday, we drove to North Wales and met up
with the other squadrons in a rotting shed, called, for the purposes
of the exercise, a war RV. At two o'clock in the morning we
moved out of the shed in our separate patrols and began a two-hour
walk across the mountains. We carried full kit including a radio set,
binoculars, a night-sight, a machine gun, chicken wire, hessian and
camouflage nets.

As dawn approached we rushed to hide ourselves like bats from
daylight. We constructed a hide squeezed in between a group of
pine trees by discreetly twisting a few branches and shaping a shield
from above with chicken wire and the camouflage net. The only
way of moving into and out of this nest was by painstakingly
crawling under the dense trees and across the carpet of sharp pine
needles. Before we had adequately finished our hide we crawled,
like the nocturnal animals we were, back into cover.

During the day we took it in turns to sleep. Two men stayed
awake and kept watch, while the other three slept. At one point
there was a mock NBC attack, when Birch dropped a number of
smoke grenades randomly around the woods. Then we had to
struggle, in seconds, into our NBC suits. We fought against
tiredness to stay awake, fearing that if we fell asleep, we would

slowly and silently suffocate inside our respirators. Outside our shelter and the pine forest, the sun shone brilliantly. I longed to escape and to stretch my legs on the hills, but we were confined, caged in by daylight.

At seven o'clock in the evening we prepared to move. We left the woods and moved tactically and in patrol formation to a new war RV. We walked, as we had done on the way to interrogation, in shadow and dead ground. When we arrived at the specified barn, we were hot and weary after a five-hour scramble across the countryside. Birch sat with the OC around an oil lamp and gave the order, 'No move before 02.00.' I lay down on the damp concrete floor and slipped into a very deep sleep.

The repeated noise of people pacing around woke me at ten minutes to two. I was stiff with cold. The concrete, like a cold temperature sink, had drawn almost all of the warmth from me. I ached and shivered, and stood up on nervous energy alone.

Birch gave orders for a dawn attack on a farm building. The farm itself was five or six kilometres away. Our patrol was designated the rear protection group and it was our job to provide covering fire for the assault team: Avery's patrol. Since Cordwell and Fowkes had gone, and Wood had been dropped from the course, Birch had merged their two patrols. Avery, Brown, Sampson and the two survivors from Three and Four Squadrons made up the second patrol. Fatty, Jim, Will, Gordon and I made up the first. Spike split the five of us in One Squadron up into two groups: Charlie and Delta, and each group carried a machine gun. Fatty and I made up the Charlie group.

We walked with Avery's patrol for two hours, in darkness, and over some foothills. At one point we had to cross a river but it was just possible to wade, and not so deep that we had to swim across. But even with the water stopping at our chests it was bitterly cold. We crossed obstacle after obstacle before finally stopping on the crest of a hill overlooking a small valley. Will, Jim and Gordon walked on the same contour around the head of the valley, and concealed themselves, opposite us, on the far side. A small stream, flowing through a deep V-shaped bank, cascaded down the centre.

Avery's patrol moved forwards in twos and threes, just as Brown, Ham and I had moved on Camp when approaching a solitary sniper. But, unlike us, they moved in silence. The isolated dwelling stood, like a mill, just to the side of the stream. I erected the machine gun, leaving Fatty, who had the binoculars, to the right of a group of boulders. He was watching for the signal to fire.

We had thousands of blank rounds between us and our orders were to capture the farmhouse and any occupants. We suspected Falstaff would be inside and he would have to be dragged out onto the grass and searched. In times of war he could, the OC said, be an enemy agent, or even guilty of hiding alien troops, just as the Italian hill farmers had concealed British soldiers during the Second World War.

When the signal came, with the first flicker of light, I squeezed the trigger and the jagged sweep of machine-gun fire cut through the silence like a chain saw. The Delta group did the same and the valley resounded with the rattle of blank rounds. Avery's patrol swooped down on the farmhouse, like vultures falling on a corpse, and for a few minutes we stopped firing.

Within seconds Falstaff was lying face down on the grass, with Sampson's automatic weapon a few feet from his head. Avery heaved him over onto his side. When he had been searched and the signal given, we slipped down the hillside to join up with Avery's patrol immediately behind the farm. There we reorganized, and made good any man's deficiency in ammunition with our own. We moved off quickly, leaving Falstaff on his back outside his farm.

Within half an hour, we were walking into the transient colours of dawn. Where there had been rapid fire there was now peace: the silence after an attack. The wet grass reflected the red hues in the sky. Darkness left us as suddenly as it came. Like vampires satisfied during the night, we swept back across the hills before we too should be caught in the sunlight. Our day was over. Now we sought rest.

'What are you thinking, sir?' Hassan asked, as we walked back along the sands. Bright red crabs scurried aside at our approach, disappearing down holes in the beach. When we had passed they would emerge again, their blank, protruding white eyes following every step.

'It could have been such a waste,' I said, 'and for nothing. What did you say to them?'

'I said you worked for the Government, sir, and if they killed you, the Government would come looking for them. But they didn't listen.'

We walked fast along the sands, alive with crabs. There were thousands and thousands of them all the same, like crowds emerging from a subway, spilling out onto the ground. They were a pure blood-red. They had no camouflage and they made no attempt to confuse. They speckled the beach far into the distance, giving the white sands the appearance of splattered sheets.

'We must go to the bazaar, sir, and buy some guns or some knives. It is not safe to go with nothing. I can use a knife. I am not afraid.'

We moved in arrowhead formation, stretching right across the valley, weapons at the ready, and silhouetted against a fiery red skyline.

I looked at my watch. It was six-thirty. We had been tense and busy for forty-eight hours. The exercise was over. I took the lead and sat on my bergen in the sun outside the war RV. Gradually, the others followed. Idly, like Falstaff's soldiers, we cleaned our weapons.

LOOKING FOR DIAMONDS

Action is famous, accomplishment is happy,
and the privilege of doing a thing well and
intently is a salve for a myriad injuries.
      Edmund Blunden on Thomas Hardy

Five days later, on the Friday before the badging weekend, I sat on a comfortable chair in Harrods, waiting for my barber to return from lunch.

'Ah, Mr Ballinger,' he said, as he came up to me. 'I'm afraid this is the last time I shall be able to cut your hair.'

'Are you leaving?' I asked.

'Yes,' he said. 'We're being privatized. The boss has sold off the barber's shop.'

'You're joking.'

'I wish I was.'

After a good bit of my hair had been removed we began talking about the army.

'I've been in the reserves for a couple of years,' I said, 'but I don't know whether to stay or to go. It's a hard decision. I don't think I'm a born soldier, but I'll miss it if I go.'

'Ah,' he said, ceasing to snip my hair and looking at me in the mirror, 'the war taught me a similar lesson. You know for all that, a lot of us didn't make good soldiers, but afterwards we made bloody good civilians.'

*

That evening the other four squadrons came to our barracks for the final test weekend. All that now separated us from entrance into 21 SAS was one thousand metres of water, which we had to swim across in our clothes, and three exams, each with one written and one practical paper. One of the papers was on chemical warfare, another on first aid, and the third was a general paper, covering such topics as navigation, patrolling, techniques in an ambush and the different types of foreign weapons.

On Saturday morning, when we were warming up for our jog to the swimming pool, the OC called us together. 'At the end of today, lads, if you pass, you will be admitted into this regiment and the Colonel will be here to give you your berets. It's a fucking great honour, lads. There's nothing in life like it. You'll never forget today. It's a landmark in a man's life.'

It was still dark but the barrack-square was floodlit.

'But listen, lads. Entry does not imply acceptance. It's hard to get into this regiment – fucking hard. But it's even harder to stay in it. Three years, that's what it takes, just to be accepted. You've got to prove yourselves.

'Good luck today, lads. Think clearly and remember everything you've been taught. I hope I will see all ten of you tonight, for the badging ceremony.

'OK. Your PSI will now take you to the pool for the final swim test.'

We jogged to the pool and after the swim test Birch led us, for the last time, on a four-mile run.

The day moved quickly between written and practical exams and at six o'clock we sat around in the grubby classroom nervously awaiting our results. Birch kept us waiting unnecessarily, playing with our nerves. Rumours circulated of men who fell, like tired racehorses, at the last hurdle. An hour later Birch came in smiling and pinned up our scores on a black notice-board. No one had failed on the last day.

A few minutes later I stood, like all the other men, rigid and to attention, staring as blankly as I could, at the Roll of Honour on the front wall. The Colonel handed out berets to ten men and for the first time in my life I held the 'Who Dares Wins' badge in my hand. I looked down quickly at my prize and then back at the Colonel. No man spoke.

'Well done, lads,' the Colonel said. 'It's fucking hard to get into this regiment. But as your OC's already told you, it's even harder to stay in it. But well done – bloody well done.

'I've done some statistics and the results will interest you. Thirty per cent of you will leave within three years. One of you will go on to command a squadron and one of you will disgrace himself, and be dismissed from the regiment, within the first year.

'In times of war you have an extremely important role and during the Second World War more men came from the reserves than from the regular army. You are vital. I know some of you have got good brains. Use them. You will not be disappointed with this regiment.'

We were dismissed and invited into the sergeants' mess for drinks. Spike was there and so was Scott and they both shook me by the hand. So too were Gordon, Fatty, Jim and Will, and in One Squadron, Avery, Brown and Sampson. Looking around inquisitively, I saw for the first time a portrait in oils of Paddy Mayne, one of the very distinguished members of the wartime regiment. Birch, seeing me stare at the painting, handed me a pint of beer.

'How do you feel?' he asked.

'Embarrassed, really,' I said. 'I've walked across the hills and listened to a series of lectures. I still feel I know nothing about soldiering.'

Birch stopped smiling. 'Good. As long as you realize that.' But then after an uncomfortable pause, the smile returned and he said, 'Hill walking does, however, have an uncanny way of sorting men out.'

At this, Falstaff, who had come back to enjoy a free drink, walked over to us, sloshing his ale on the floor as he did so. Hill walking was his domain. Men who passed his course went on to Camp and then, if they survived that, on to Birch.

'Finding the right men,' said Falstaff, 'is like looking for diamonds. During Selection we knock away the bad rock until a rough diamond is found. Camp is a cutting process when we chip off the bad edges. Continuation is the polish. It's our job to present clean diamonds to the regiment.'

'Can you spot the diamonds, in the rock, before the course begins?' I asked.

'Yes, I can,' said Falstaff, his eyes twinkling. 'It's all in the eyes, and the mind. You remember having your photograph taken at the beginning of the course?'

'On attestation?'

'Yes. We put them all together on a big sheet of cardboard. I've got a black pen and we cross out every face that will fail. Ninety-five per cent of the time we're right. It's interesting to see them fall. Sometimes we put money on it. I can even tell when some of them will go. You can look at a man and say, "He'll fail on weekend four, he'll fail on Long Drag and he'll fail on TQ." You escaped the black pen, but Sampson is a surprise. We thought he'd fail. Most muscle men do.'

I looked over Falstaff's shoulder and saw, not twenty feet away, standing at the bar, the man I had met on the Pennines. He was in uniform talking to the Colonel. I was so shocked I hesitated to move, but I had often thought about him. I excused myself quickly and began to cross the mess but it was crowded with lots of soldiers and officers accompanying the Colonel. When I arrived at the bar he had gone. I rushed into the hall, but that too was empty. There were any number of doors through which he might have passed, but it was not my place to try them. I wanted so much to talk to him, but he had gone, just as quietly as he had left the train in Derby station. 'You'll do it,' he had said two years ago. "How does he know?" I remembered asking myself at the time.

About midnight the Colonel and his officers left the mess and only Birch and the ten of us remained. But soon after, recruits started to leave in ones and twos. Birch continued to drink but he never sat down. He stood tall and straight and walked from the bar to the buffet talking to each man in turn.

'What do you do now Continuation is over, sir?' I asked, when he came up to me again.

'I go back to Hereford next week,' he said. 'I've got a few more years yet. But after that I don't know.'

One by one we sat down on the padded chairs. Will and Jim came up to me and were just about to drag me onto the floor when Will tripped and fell, drunk, onto a coffee table. Birch laughed and walked out.

Avery sat down beside me and, spilling his beer, set his glass on the table. He was shaking.

'I've given everything I fucking had for this,' he said, pulling his new beret from his pocket. 'Look at it, just look at it. A piece of fucking cloth. That's all it is.' He squeezed the badge and said, 'It's not even two inches square.' Avery picked up his drink and his arm wavered. He lifted his glass to his mouth and poured, but he tipped it so quickly that the beer ran out around his cheeks and spilt on his shirt.

Will and Jim came swaying back across the mess and started to tease him. Avery had never liked them and he stood up immediately. Jim pushed him on the shoulder and Will moved to trip him up, but Avery stepped forward and picked up his beer glass. He raised his arm as if to push the glass into Jim's face.

'Avery!' I said, jumping up. 'If Birch sees you you're finished.'

'Come on, Will,' said Jim. 'Let's bugger off.'

Avery and I were left alone in the mess. The others had already gone. We sat back down and I looked at my watch: it was nearly four in the morning.

Avery stared at me, his eyes watering.

THE SINAI

Are you, then, so easily turned from your design? Did you not call this a glorious expedition? And wherefore was it glorious? Not because the way was smooth and placid as a southern sea, but because it was full of dangers and terror, because at every new incident your fortitude was to be called forth and your courage exhibited, because danger and death surrounded it, and these you were to brave and overcome. For this it was glorious, for this it was an honourable undertaking . . . Oh! Be men, or be more than men. Be steady to your purposes and firm as rock.

Mary Shelley

A few months later I made my way, as I had to, through the chain of command, and asked for leave of absence.

For two years I had given everything I possessed to a single cause. I had trained for nearly three hours a day, running or cycling on average about ten miles, and swimming a further mile. I wanted a rest and then time off to get married.

When I found the OC, in the squadron barracks, he was busy cooking his dinner on a portable stove. I explained my circumstances.

'I'm getting married in two months,' I said.

'Carry on,' he said.

'I might move to Devon afterwards.'

He looked down, wistfully, at his sweetcorn. For a second I feared the worst, but then he raised his head and looked straight at me. 'There's no squadron location in Devon,' he began, 'and any commitment will put your marriage at risk. You would spend your life on British Rail.' He stopped pushing his sweetcorn around the saucepan and looked down into the boiling water. 'You are trying to decide between doing this and preserving your marriage: no man should have to make that decision.' He lifted his dinner off the cooker and placed it alongside the sink. For a few seconds neither of us spoke and then, taking out the pad of paper he kept in his top left pocket, he scribbled down a few details.

The permission was granted with immediate effect.

Walking away from me, he scanned a calendar on the white-washed wall and looked dubiously into the future. 'Think about it,' he said. 'Contact me in the autumn.' I thanked him and as I turned to go he called out, 'Ballinger—'

'Yes, sir?' I said.

'Enjoy your honeymoon.'

I walked down the familiar stairs and out onto the barrack-square. On the inside of the running track the 10th Gurkha Rifles were celebrating their centenary. I stood quiet and alone to watch. A little man, smartly dressed and on guard, came up to me. He was in the 7th Gurkha Rifles, The Duke of Edinburgh's Own. His father had served in the same regiment. I stood with him for a while and together we listened to the band and the music, and watched the pomp and circumstance. At the end of the celebrations I walked towards the gatehouse. The little Gurkha waved. I raised my hand and smiled. It could have been a salute but it was not.

A week later I caught a bus from the Abbassya Terminal in Cairo to the Sinai Desert.

As we raced across the sands I sat glued to the window, fascinated by the rapidly changing scene. I was happy: I was travelling again. From the deep blue hues of the Suez Canal and the Red Sea we moved into a land of even fewer colours; where the stark mountains soared upwards towards a burning sun; where the ground was lacerated with trenches giving it the appearance of a messy wound.

Sheets of corrugated iron glistened in the sunlight. Barbed wire, tangled like briars in a blackberry bush, lay across the trenches. Deserted bunkers hideously deformed by high explosives, from the inside out, had been left to bake in the sun. Telltale signs of conflict, carcasses of war.

I got off the bus in a small village a dozen miles before St Catherine's.

For four days I trekked with a guide in the mountains. We picked our way along tiny tracks that I would never have found, over the barren terrain. For days we saw no one else. The mountains were awesome and the heat forbidding. And yet as we climbed and walked along the jagged ridges of massive red-brown cliffs I felt a curious peace. I was no longer racing against a clock, struggling onwards against a wintry headwind to the next RV. I was walking slowly and carefully. For a while I tried to construct a selection course, in my mind, on this terrain, but it was beyond me.

On the fifth day, at dawn, we packed up our belongings and separated. I left my guide in the mosque on the summit of Mount Sinai, and walked alone down to St Catherine's Monastery.

One night a French Catholic monk, who had spent the last forty years in Mauritania, invited me to join him for dinner. We sat on the hot sand behind the monastery, leaning, in the darkness, on some pale blue cushions. I gazed up at the stars. They did not quite begin at the horizon as I had been led to believe, but they were close enough. The moon was one-quarter full and the Plough was clearer than I had seen it before. A resplendent silver tray of food arrived and we ate.

The devout man continued to eat long after I had finished, but when he too had satisfied his appetite the tray was removed and tea was brought. I played with my thimble-sized cup of sweet tea, sat quietly, and listened to his stories of Christians in Mauritania. Our little candle flickered in the cool night air. Soon it would burn itself out. Time was slipping by. Two small feet padded towards us, through the sands.

*

'I am going back to the room now, sir,' Hassan said. 'I am very tired now. I want to sleep.'

'Here,' I said. 'Take the key.'

'What will you do, sir?'

'I'll come back later.'

With a puff our candle was extinguished, and we surrendered our cushions and glasses. We got up and walked back towards the monastery slowly, and parted at the gate.